Journey into Journalism

Other works by Arnold Wesker:

Plays
The Kitchen
The Wesker Trilogy:
   Chicken Soup with Barley
   Roots
   I'm Talking about Jerusalem
Chips With Everything
Menace (Television Play)
The Four Seasons
Their Very Own and Golden City
The Friends
The Old Ones
The Journalists
The Wedding Feast
The Merchant

Essays and Short Stories
Fears of Fragmentation
Six Sundays in January
Love Letters on Blue Paper (also a television and
   stage play)
Say Goodbye: You May Never See Them Again (text
   with paintings by John Allin)
Words — as Definitions of Experience

Arnold Wesker's work has been translated into
thirteen languages and produced in over fifty
countries.

Journey into Journalism

A very personal account in four parts

by Arnold Wesker

Note: All quotations are from journalists most of whom, I think, would want to remain anonymous.

Writers and Readers Publishing Cooperative

© 1977 Arnold Wesker

Published by Writers and Readers Publishing Cooperative
233a Kentish Town Road, London NW5 2JT

Printed in Great Britain by Redwood Burn Limited,
Trowbridge and Esher

ISBN 0 904613 68 2 (casebound)
ISBN 0 904613 53 4 (paperback)

Contents

Preface—1972

There was a moment when I seriously considered not publishing this small book because the material for it was gathered for another reason: as a background setting for my play *The Journalists*. It seemed I was cheating.

I had asked, and was generously granted, permission to wander freely through the offices of The Sunday Times. But I couldn't resist shaping the notes made there into a piece of journalism. Surely, even if no one published it, the organisation of scrawl into a coherent shape would assist in the writing of the play. It did. Fortunately, my publisher also liked it.

Although most of the quotations came from journalists working on The Sunday Times some do not. It would be too pedantic to distinguish who said what, nor does it matter. I wanted to evoke a newspaper atmosphere as well as describe particular events — and so I've chosen this mixed form, of sequence and montage; sometimes the record is chronological, sometimes one passage draws together many statements uttered at different times by different people.

I'm very indebted to Harry Evans, the editor. He didn't think it incumbent upon me to ask for permission to publish it but it was important to me to receive his blessing before agreeing to let my publisher go ahead. He gave it despite having, naturally, very strong criticisms. Considering that I became simply another headache added to all those confronting an editor he has been courteous (if firm about certain aspects of the piece), helpful and finally very just.

London
July 1972

Preface—1977

Since writing that first preface, almost five years ago, a great deal has happened. So much that inevitably one asks is it too late for the book to be published? I don't know but wish to take the risk. A book on journalism is/was the largest writ invitation to criticism, but because publication was held up there is the added risk of anti-climax: what was all the fuss about?

An explanation of the delay is necessary. On pages 21 to 34 I've written the story within the story, of how I got certain things wrong and was sternly corrected. I've not only recorded the telling off but have shown how I went wrong and added the corrections in the critics' own words — my mistakes and the manner in which they were corrected were, after all, also part of my 'journey into journalism'.

These additions failed to satisfy, or pacify, at least two of the journalists on the staff. I made a vow to myself that, because I'd gained entry into the building in order to collect material for a play, I'd publish only if everyone with whom I'd spoken agreed I could publish the slim volume. It was a self-imposed restriction. For five years the objections remained. Then in a T.V. interview with Melvyn Bragg, when asked in connection with freedom of the press "What about the Wesker book?" Harry Evans implied there were no longer any reasons why it shouldn't be published. He turned to the camera and said "You can go ahead and publish, Arnold!"

I do so, and offer the work with the words of the late Nick Tomalin:

"You got it as right as any of us ever get anything right!"

London
January 1977

7

Part One

"There's no role for this country to perform, so where do the best minds go? Not politics or the civil service — journalism instead. They can't legislate or exercise power so — they comment! Journalism as an act of creating self-awareness in society."

The beginning

I have been told "you can come any time, sit in, see anything." The purpose: I'm contemplating writing a play with a newspaper background. The Times Diary hear of the story and a reporter 'phones me to ask the odd gossipy question, I tell him I want to avoid creating a cliche setting. Some days later they write up the story and invent a quote: "He (Wesker) calls his stint 'living in the atmosphere of printers ink' — that's a cliche he might avoid . . ." I wince at the lie but am reminded why I want to write the play.

The reception area is designed by Lord Snowdon out of blocks and lines of type-face in different sizes. The lights over the desks and interviewing tables hang down low enough for you to crack your head. On the walls of corridors is marshalled the faded past: yellowing prints* once upon a time produced for the popular inquisitiveness of Sunday Times readers; old imaginations peeling off walls where new ones labour to invent fresh sheets for mass curiosity. In the editor's office, my first stop, is a full sized pop painting with books on one wall and furnishings in red leather. Instructions have been given to take me to Fleet Street's El Vino.

On the way my guide, one of Fleet Street's tough and

* Interiors may, of course, have changed in five years. Inevitably many similar parts of this document are 'history'. To change it all would have involved a new tour. I hope such preteritions will be minimal and viewed as secondary to the main body of the work.

feared men ("I have no emotions whatsoever") casually recalls this story. "You may not remember, but I used to work for a magazine and one day we sent my wife to interview you. A hatchet job. Let's get at the truth of this man, we thought, he must be a phoney, him and his Centre 42. But she came back saying 'I can't, I can't! He's genuine, talked to me like an equal.' It was a good piece finally." He's the first of a team of highly intelligent and complex personalities I'm to meet in the course of my researches, a man responsible for unearthing some of the seediest manipulators of our competitive society.

El Vino is full of men without women. No woman is allowed to buy a drink at the bar.* We make for the back where a large, red-streaked nose man seems to be holding court. He throws open his arms at me and says, "I want to speak with *that* man." Thank God my dull brain for names is working. He's a theatre reviewer — lovely man, careless critic. It looks as though wit and anecdotes are about to buzz, but little happens. I'm relieved, the pressure to be funny is always depressing. There's an atmosphere of shabby, besotted agitation where consolations and praises are passed between moist lips; a place where, I feel, reporters tell each other the real truth and share their weariness of the world. I don't know what I'm supposed to feel but attempt to feel it. Soon I'm drunk and trying not to show it. Later we eat spaghetti across the road joined by three other journalists called along by my guide to help him out with his not very forthcoming guest: a literary editor — quiet and retiring as though fearful of being caught too friendly with a literary man; an Eastern European correspondent, nicely modest and full of questions; and a freelance

* Despite the Sex Discrimination Act this still operates. Speaking for El Vino after a failed recent attempt to object to their licence being renewed, Mr R.F. Tovey was quoted in The Times, 26th March 1977: "I hope you can think, as far as the ladies are concerned, that these practices are done in a manner of old world common courtesy and decency and not as a matter of discrimination. If it is discrimination, it is in their favour."

who, he reminds me later, had interviewed me for television six years ago and I'd forgotten. He works hard to extinguish my embarrassment.

My guide ends his tour at the Wig and Pen club where, quite drunk, I make some observation which wins his admiration. "There," he says, "I've been with you all day and I've been wondering — what makes this man talented? He's not very witty, a bit reticent — but wham! You come out with an observation like that and I realise — that's his genius." He confirms my fear that I'm expected to produce instant brilliance and I'm relieved to find I'd accidentally let slip at least one bright remark.

"Journalists write for other journalists, the people they have lunch with rather than the reader. Except for political journalists — they write for politicians. Who knows what the reader wants? One of the reasons newspapers are always running opinion polls is that they don't know what the reader thinks."

Editorial conference

The atmosphere is casual, relaxed. They wear a mixture of clothing: pink shirts and red ties, smart lawyer suits, pin stripes, sports jackets. It reflects assorted backgrounds. Old hands and young academics; some from provincial papers, others from the rough hustling of defunct popular dailies. Everyone seems to have read all the papers before 9 a.m. and listened to everything on radio and T.V. My problem in the beginning is I can't hear what they're saying because I'm so absorbed by the way they're saying it.

"What are we going to do about Bengal this week?"

The editor lifts the internal 'phone to the sports

editor. "Hello, John? Yesterday's Financial Times. Page 12. Second column, three up from the bottom. Aston Villa football club is offering you, me and others shareholdings in the club. Might make a good story for 'Inside Track'. Who is selling them, how many, why and who's buying? OK?" He puts down the receiver and sparkles at a colleague: "You going to listen to us and put the papers down and stop reading?"

"Yes, when you've stopped 'phoning." The conference begins.

"The trouble is we're all in agreement that we're right and they're wrong."

"Oh, I don't know, I'm more inflationary than you."

"Are you? Well *you're* wrong then. What about the rest of the government's strategy? I think we're entitled to be absolutely critical of all aspects by now and it would be absolutely consistent with our policy of criticism throughout."

"There *is* no economic strategy."

"But there is a philosophy. I mean 'let lame ducks go to the wall and stand on your own two feet' *is* a philosophy."

"Yes, but it's not a strategy."

"Where are we on Soyuz?"

"No further than any other newspaper."

"I thought the Daily Mail did it very well this morning, very well indeed."

"Maybe, but I didn't like all that science fiction writing."

"Oh, I thought that was interesting, I liked that. Do we know why the monkey died last time?"

"Boredom I think."

"What about the escaped Soviet space scientist?"

"Who's got his head at the moment?"

"Foreign Office isn't it?"

"Can he be got at?"

"Put in an official request I think."

"I think you'd better do that."

"OK. I will, although the rumour is that he doesn't know one end of a space craft from another and that in fact he's a ballistics expert."

The News Editor raises the issue of high explosives hidden in the Welsh mountains, he thinks it's a danger and that the local population ought to be told; but apparently the government have slapped a 'D' notice on it and he's told: "It may be a 'D' notice we ought to respect. After all we don't want the other side to know where we keep our bombs and we all know there's a lot of mad Irishmen running around trying to get their hands on some high explosives."

Confronted with how much news *isn't* used I realise now, if I hadn't realised it before, the amount of news which the media pour out. And I begin wondering to what extent journalists are aware of how they inundate people with information about events which depress and confuse them while not at the same time offering a way out from feelings of impotence. And are they conscious that news has become a marketable commodity to whose 'packaging', like all commodities, special attention must be paid? Do they constantly question themselves, scrutinise their decisions in order to maintain a delicate balance between the demands to decorate the package and the responsibility to present it accurately? Not always easy. Accuracy may be boring, too complex, often bewilderingly contradictory. Contradictions in a complex world must be a difficult commodity to sell.

"Poor Arnold, this must be frustrating for you, not being able to say anything and listening to us pass judgements and decide our opinions in five minutes on major issues. But we've worked together a long time now; what you're hearing is the result of hours spent talking on these issues at other times." It doesn't help.

> "The Sunday Times? It's no a newspaper, more an adventure playground for journalists."

Amblings

I wander around. People stop and talk to me. I feel intimidated but don't let it be seen; instead I shamelessly allow my reputation to go before me. They don't guess that I don't know what I'm looking for or what questions to ask. The men I meet are fast thinking, knowledgeable, have firsts from Oxbridge or scars from searing experiences around the world. And they all exude that quality of being 'good and honourable men'. But to them I'm 'the artist', a 'magic man' who can, without actually knowing, see the truth behind the facade, the devil in the making. I feel them behave in special ways in my presence. My advantage is doubled: what they suspect are my special powers of perception plus the fact — which I enjoy — that it's they instead of me who are under scrutiny. My disadvantage is the problem of disentangling the truth from the performance they're giving. "That's the problem of the reporter," I'm told, "and you're facing it in the presence of the best performers in the business." My aim is to be unobtrusive, shadowy. Occasionally, inspired, I phrase the right question; mostly, they credit me with having asked the right question and simply talk. My external demeanour, hopefully, is cool and assured. Secretly I'm startled at the speed with which they grasp the drift of my doubts, confused by the shorthand language they adopt to communicate ideas among themselves, and frequently overwhelmed by the incomprehensible technical vocabulary they call upon whether dealing with economics, diplomatic affairs or our technical times.

We chat in odd corners, on the stairs, in the pub at lunch time, and I sense a genuine, disarming eagerness to reveal, justify. "I suppose in my field I'm among the top three in Fleet Street" says one in response to a question from me about his future. I find it an honest, innocent reply. I believe him. But what would he have done with such a statement from me? He'd have gone to town on that one, a juicy quote to reveal the conceit of his victim.

15

Everyone laughs loudly at his own jokes. "Have you noticed," someone asks over lunch, "how we all flatter each other?" "No," I reply, "but I've noticed how you all *wait* for each other's flattery." My wit is ignored, which hurts since it's so rare; and he continues. "I went to play tennis with someone from the business page who'd just investigated Hitachi or some such - I'd never read the business page, who does? - but I did it for that game so that I was able to say between balls 'I didn't think you'd been to Japan last month.' "

Their conversation is rapid and their laughter covers the common ground of mutually recognised foibles or the in-tales of other Fleet Street journalists. "Wilson said of her or was it Crossman?: 'Political journalist? That bitch would get a scoop wrong if you gave it to her at dictation speed.' " I have difficulty in stretching my smile to cover all their funnies, a great many of which are delivered in the shorthand of a shared working experience that's unfamiliar to me. I'm told, and must remember, that when in editorial conferences they argue for space and seem not to be taking anything seriously it's because they have to represent their story in caricature terms in order not to be caught being serious, which would be an invitation to derision. Seriousness, they assure me, appears while they're discussing and canvassing for support in the corridors - - as with any establishment possessing power. Why does seriousness invite derision? Pomposity, yes. Is that what is meant? Do journalists have difficulty in being serious without being pompous?

I experience, then, their desperate need to be found witty — a highly prized and regarded attribute, demonstrating, I suppose, the cool detachment they feel is required for the sober assessment of news. Or is it that immured in what they see as the ghastly spectacle world news presents of man's stupidity and inhumanity they're forced to develop wit as a safety valve? Whatever, it's not easy to sustain an appreciative grin for a whole day, every day, and I can never be quite certain whether the wit is a safety valve against the world's horrors or against suspicions of their impotence to do anything about it.

One of the issues agitating them in my first week is the publication of Eysenck's book, "Race, Intelligence and Education". Everyone wants to attack it. "I mean look at this paragraph: 'Nearly every anatomical, physiological and bio-chemical system investigated shows racial differences. Why should the brain be an exception?' Well," they explode, "why *shouldn't* it? *Nearly* every system shows racial differences he says. Well if *not* 'every' why not make a point of *that*? And if *'nearly* every' then how can he ask 'why should the brain be an exception?' It's such unscientific thinking and writing that makes me so suspicious of the man."

I read a transcript of a conversation three journalists have had with Eysenck. One of the questions asked is: 'could you be accused of erring according to Liam Hudson's law of selective attention to data?' It seems an odd question to be asked by a journalist whose profession is entirely given to just that, selecting data. "Public figures are in danger of complacency," says one journalist, "so need to be continually liable to attack. The hunting pleasure, though I don't approve of it, is one of the satisfactions of journalism."

But not only does the journalist's work appear every day multiplying the law of 'selective attention to data', he also seems to assume his individual power is minimal without taking into account the power residing in the *totality* of the press. Who curbs the greater sense of complacency that must come from that? Who will hunt, probe and attack the strange motives *he* may have?

> "The journalist claims and exercises the moral right to expose other individuals whose moral righteousness they suspect."

Insight

It's a strange name to give a column. What can it mean? In-depth? Probe? Mystical illumination? The word suggests a virtue usually claimed by literature which has time to explore contradictions and paradoxes and be subtly perceptive about them. Can a newspaper do and be these things?

Their office has a large print of Mao on the wall and a poster saying 'Women of Britain say — GO! 1920', rather like photographs of nudes which boys hang in their rooms at public school to assert their independence while temporarily trapped by the enemy. But I'm assured that's not the case: "I bought it as a pure piece of art — the design of propaganda art interests me deeply." Everyone is young, surely under thirty, and seems to care.

Insight, I'm told, has created journalistic history: the detailed and complicated investigative reporting of issues and scandals of a public, social and political nature, a procedure "often involving confrontation with very difficult people". Normally a newspaper is laid out on the basis of a number of assumptions: a) the reader's intellectual limitations — big print, short, snappy articles, a photographic profusion of breasts, thighs, action; b) the reader's sexual appetites and voyeuristic inclinations — cover the law courts for cases of rape, adultery, vicarage orgies; c) intellectual aspirations — wide arts coverage, diaries of politicians, international news concerning industrial development; d) the place where the paper is likely to be read — in a train to and from work, at leisure by the breakfast teapot, in the lounge on a Sunday morning, and so on. But until the advent of Insight it seemed that every newspaper from the so-called pops to the so-called heavies, agreed that (wherever they individually gauged it) all newspaper readers did have a saturation point, a kind of text sound-barrier beyond which print dizziness set in or the reader went berserk. In the News of the

World it may have been a whole page relieved by many photographs and in The Observer it may have been a whole page stubbornly stripped of photographs, but no one, it was felt, had patience or powers of concentration for more.

Insight thought differently: if the issue was important enough and if they spent more than the normal time which a trip, a chat and a bit of back-number reading involved, then there would be an intelligent readership for it. More, they were also prepared to spend the money to prove it, and did.

At my request they recite their record:

"The RB211 fiasco, how it happened and what the various governments were doing. Scandals in local government contracting. The failures in air safety regulations which led to the deaths of 72 people, unnecessarily, after their aircraft crashed and caught fire at Rijeka. Then a long account of the effects of a restrictive abortion policy in Birmingham which, because senior doctors in the area disapproved, led to disastrous medical decisions such as refusing to abort German measle babies. Then a long and sympathetic analysis of Wilson's efforts to hold Labour together over the EEC, by far the most detailed, and kindest, to appear. Then Northern Ireland, internment, we moved over there and remained for almost a year involved in much patient and occasionally risky work, confronting massed public opinion . . ."

It's impressive. Some people find their tone self-righteous, and confronting them is a bit like walking towards a policeman — the knowledge of his function makes you feel guilty for something or other. But they seem to have no pretentions about being authorities on the world and if their articles finally give the impression that they've become instant experts on everything, this results more from the unavoidably persuasive power of print than it reflects their own delusions.

In my week with them they are investigating falling bridges but, it seems, with scant enthusiasm. "This subject must have priority over something, though God knows what!" The impression of indifference is a false one, the result of a strange journalistic disease they call 'hyping' (from the Greek word 'hyperbole' which first came into the English language in about 1529 and means 'exaggeration'). Behind the shorthand of jokes and the contrived casualness is the reading, they tell me, of a lot of technical reports, innumerable consultations with construction experts and midnight meetings between themselves and Sunday Times technical experts.

I don't see any of this. It takes place in other rooms and at other hours. What I see are four people on the telephone at once; it's difficult to follow all their conversations but it's obvious that at this stage they don't know anything about their subject. With disarming honesty they 'phone around for enlightenment.

"Professor Wells in Belfast please . . . Professor Wells? Ah, good morning, Insight Sunday Times here. Look, I don't know how to start thinking on this subject at all — yes, the fallen bridges, you've guessed it — I don't know what are the questions to ask nor in what order nor who can answer them or how you set them up. Can I ring you again when I've worked out some basic shape to the piece and ask you whether it makes engineering sense?"

Another member of the team is making a brave attempt to understand, he's onto a ministry official.

"I'm very much a layman so if I could explain in layman's language rather than your usual language of expertise . . . but as I understand it, it goes something like this: I build shelves for 15lb jam jars, test the shelves by putting 20lb jam jars on, use 15lb jam jars for 20 years and then return to 20lb jam jars . . . Oh! I see. Jam jars are hardly applicable. Of course. Well, let's start again . . ."

They nurse each other's incomprehensions.

"As far as I can make out it's a perfectly decent feat

of engineering but no one seems to have taken account of the fact that the things are built by incompetent, lumpen Irish labourers who don't care a damn."

Someone tells me an Insight anecdote:

"You know, the Conservative Party thinks The Sunday Times is Maoist and The Times merely left wing. I was talking to this woman, Mrs O, and she whispered to me: 'I think you've got three full card paying members of the Communist Party on your Insight team.' And I said to her, 'Oh no! They're not as right wing as that'."

A bottle of wine arrives. The People column have sent it. It seems departments send gifts to staff colleagues who supply them with a story. People gives wine, Atticus gives whisky.

Loyalties to sources of information present problems for journalists. Insight investigated the collapse of the Vehicle & General Insurance Company and found from a high-ranking contact in the Board of Trade that they'd known about the company's precarious condition but had received directives from the government not to enquire further, as the Tories were pursuing a 'hands off industry' policy. At the tribunal investigating the V. & G.'s collapse, the reporter was called as a witness and asked to reveal his source of information. He refused which left the tribunal able to dismiss his evidence as mere hearsay, thus undermining the impact of The Sunday Times' investigation. They also have to grapple with the law of slander which prevents a reporter asking a question designed to find out if unsavoury assertions are true; a double-edged law which helps the citizen protect his private life and hampers the journalist who wishes to expose it to view — a good thing; or put another way: a law which helps the swindler to keep his activities secret and hampers the journalist who wants to expose it — a bad thing.

My interpretation of this law becomes a cornerstone in a stern conflict which arises between Insight and myself. When an early draft of this *Journey* appears some of the team are very distressed to find I've written

anything at all about my stay at The Sunday Times and
their reactions range from irritation at certain facts I've
got wrong or omitted, to courteous fury that I'd set out
to create, as they see it, an image of "shallow-minded
shits — who make fools of themselves on complex
matters of genuine public concern such as unsafe
bridges . . ."

Basically the protests come from three quarters:
Insight themselves are mainly concerned that I've got
facts wrong in a way which cruelly misrepresents their
function:

> "Does the sort of brutal, vulgar approach you present
> — and it is just that — really sort with our record?"

One of the managing editors who had been closely
associated with Insight is upset by the overall image and
imagines I'd only ever intended to write this diary and
therefore claimed their attention under false pretences:

> "Did you really think that because you managed to
> prevail upon Harry's generosity, that this gave you
> a licence to say what you like about anyone
> employed by The Sunday Times? Do you really
> think that when a man goes to work for a company,
> that he surrenders his reputation into their hands?
> I find it hard to be quite sure what your moral stance
> was in your negotiations with the editor. You seem
> to have been a bit sinuous . . ."

Another journalist, who has been very helpful to me
in discussing the problems of the play, feels I've mis-
represented The Sunday Times, been inaccurate in
reporting editorial conferences and, like his colleague,
feels I've been devious:

> "You make everyone out to be ruthless, ambitious,
> clever and cynical about the stuff they are dealing
> with. That may be true of a few people. But it misses
> out large numbers of reporters and other writers who

are unruthless to the point of inertia, who do not spend their life making wittily flip remarks about anything that comes their way, and who do not possess that self-deprecatory arrogance which emerges from a lot of the voices you report. A lot of people here are very ordinary people doing reasonably well the only job they are capable of doing at all. Far from parading their self-confidence in the way you suggest, they are conscious of working low down in a vast capitalist organisation. They are intensely self-critical both about the paper and about their own efforts — a point which emerges not at all from your account, yet which is fundamental to the paper's vitality . . ."

I spend days going over my draft to see if they're right and write long letters of defence. Yes, I have made some mistakes, no I haven't made everyone out to be cynical — they're too touchy on that point — but, most important, I get furious at their suggestions of deviousness. Fortunately I've carefully filed all correspondence so it can be proved I've wanted, from the start, to send the piece to everyone for approval. It takes massive and angry letters lumbering back and forth to get them to acknowledge this. Seven pages of quarto size from one ends: ". . . You may find the tone of this letter a little sharp from time to time: however I've refrigerated my original feelings as far as possible . . ." I reply with eight and a half foolscap pages: ". . . I wish you'd have placed some of your sanctimony into the freezer along with your hot passions and spared me both . . ."

The confusion grows. Someone from The Sunday Times anonymously sends a dossier to Private Eye who ring me up for confirmation of 'suppression'. I tell them no, I've just got some facts wrong and certain people are questioning them. As usual *they* get it wrong (calling me, among other mistakes, Hampstead's leading playwright when in fact I'm Highgate's) and I'm compelled to write what they call 'Long Boring Letter' in order to set certain facts right. In the process I quote, without mentioning names, an extract from one of the angry letters to me, which act arouses further and greater anger. I seem not to be doing anything right.

But the encounter is interesting in that it produces the journalistic paranoia about which many people have spoken to me, and in that I'm forced to concede and correct mistakes and to face the curious fact that people I'd liked and a column I'd respected emerges, in my early draft, as a very thin etching indeed. It's worth going into detail.

My original draft relies mostly on observation. I *hear* them making jokes about fallen bridges — I don't *see* them ploughing through reports. I *hear* them 'phoning around for information — I don't *see* them in consultation with technical advisers. What I get from these observations, and think my original draft is communicating with approval, is the sober and responsible way the team are tackling the story. I write: ". . . it's obvious they don't know anything about their subject. With disarming honesty they 'phone around for enlightenment . . .", and it seems to me I'm pointing to a laudable quality: modesty. Look, I'm saying, they have no pretentions, they don't delude themselves that they are instant experts on bridge building but begin by admitting they know nothing and start from there. Why, after all, *should* they be experts on the world? No! they write to me: ". . . what emerges is that Insight is a technically sloppy . . . group of half-wits . . ."

It startles me at first and I'm initially hurt to be so misunderstood — especially when I'd attempted to write well of them; but on reflection I recognise that their reputation for efficient and accurate investigation is more important to them than a reputation for modest investigation. So, I add to the text, write about 'hyping' and refer to the behind-the-scenes read-throughs of heavy technical jargon with which they struggle.

But a more damaging and complex piece of misreporting seems to be my description of 'the gynaecologist affair'. My first day's guide is determined to put on a 'show' for me and I confess I see more of the show than the facts. Their calm mood has been surprising me but I'm assured that such sweet and quiet atmospheres as that hovering around the subdued investigation of tragic fallen bridges are not the rule. They even apologise that there's no story around to enable me to see them in real action. What *can* such action be? I'm soon to find out. Within hours they and their situation change. The show begins.

On Friday afternoon, at 3.30, twenty-four hours before the paper needs to be put to bed, my first day's guide comes in to ask the team if they can handle the story of a National Health Service gynaecologist who has refused a 12-year-old an abortion. She is reported as having said to the child: "If you play adult games you must expect adult consequences." A story had been written by a freelance who had structured her copy with a serious tone specially for The Sunday Times. She'd offered it to the news desk who were not all that interested, certainly not at the fee she wanted. She could have got £300 from the News of the World but was horrified at the way they wanted to handle it so she came back again to The Sunday Times one of whose other more senior editors (my guide) had got hold of it and was now lunging around demanding why the hell the story hadn't been picked up before.

But Insight are reluctant to handle it because they think it's simply another news story. The senior editor disagrees and points out that she's a National Health medical officer and paid to *help* wayward and confused children of twelve not to pass moral judgements on them. "Problem is," he says, "she's clamped down, refuses to speak to the press. What we want is the story of a guilty gynaecologist. Was she married? Did she have an unhappy love affair? Get a photograph, even if it's of her peering reluctantly round the door."

"Jesus!" Insight's editor protests, "that's Harold Robbins not journalism."

The team can see that, though there's genuine concern behind the attempt to galvanise them, nevertheless a special performance is being laid on for my benefit and they're slightly embarrassed by it. But they remain loyal, though not without protest. Another of the team insists: "It's not an Insight story at all, just a classic newsroom story. Girls of twelve, even ten are having abortions all the time." At this stage activity heightens. 'Phones slam, a news reporter is brought in. The original story is photostated and handed around. Everyone is briefed.

"You can get up to Bradford in two and a half hours on the M.1."

"Three and a half."

"Four." Suddenly it *seems* like Hollywood journalism in place of the sober assembling of news and opinion I've witnessed till now. And my first draft leaves that impression.

They protest:

"The idea that The Sunday Times heavy mob went boiling up the Motorway that night to rip all the veils from gynaecologist's psycho-social history within 24 hours is both untrue and preposterous . . ."

Watching them make their plans (even though not ones for 'boiling up the motorway') a thought crosses my mind: an unsuspecting professional citizen, culpable no doubt, is being gunned for. The hounds are being unleashed, I think; horses are mounted, blood is smelt, someone has blown the horn. I'm in a position to telephone her, warn her to put herself, her friends and her colleagues on guard, to go on holiday, underground. She may have behaved inhumanly but, so it seems, an inhuman hunt is on. My pity is aroused and conflicts with the condemnation I feel for her behaviour. Insight protest again at the way I word this. They're right. I've been mesmerised by what appears to be the coming alive of a myth in front of my eyes: The Newspaper Hunt. "Basically," calls out one reporter from the other side of the room to their galvanizer, "what you want is all the dirt we can get on the woman?" "Yes," he replies. I scribble my notes: ". . . all the dirt we can get on the woman . . ." Great copy! And it ties in with those questions: ". . . was she married? Did she have an unhappy love affair? . . ." My early draft is full of such wide-eyed discovery. But the 'hype'! the 'hype'! I'd not known about the 'hype'. The team educate me:

"It's another example of the shorthand that comes from long proximity that you didn't grasp . . . 'getting the dirt' didn't mean getting information about her sex life but her professional record . . ."

I next write about the moral implications of pursuing the gynaecologist after the affair is over but I make the mistake of doing so without asking further questions. There's great confusion. *They* think I've accused them of a callous indifference to the possibility of again distressing the mother and child by boiling up the M.1. to question them; it *could* have been read like that and, since they are suspicious of the circumstances surrounding the diary's creation and ill-disposed towards its final shape, they did! But actually I only mean to suggest that it's the reappearance of the issue in the press which will again upset them. In a letter explaining this I add what I believe to be a humorous aside: "What *is* laughable, of course, is my assumption that mother or daughter or any friend who might recognise the case would read The Sunday Times." My sociological observation is pounced upon as a "just zany sneer presumably meant to show that no warm, real working class people would ever read The Sunday Times."

It becomes one of those situations where everything I write is now misunderstood. The tone of attack and defence grow in acrimony but I make a great effort not to lose sight of the fact that I have made mistakes — the main one being my failure to check that in fact it was the mother herself who had asked a journalist to investigate the gynaecologist's behaviour; nor did I notice in the final article that no mention was made of the mother or child's name. In this way, through inexperience, I learn how, despite being around for weeks, it's easy to get a story wrong. (What of the reporter who pops in and out of a story for a few hours?)

But what I find bewildering is the vehemence of personal accusation and abuse most of which is angrily founded upon the insufficiently investigated assumption that I'd deliberately tried to get the diary published behind their backs — and this from people who were accusing me of insufficient investigation!

It depresses me. The onslaught seriously makes me think my entire first *Journey into Journalism* must be abortive. Everyone advises me to give up — "you'll never get it right, they'll always find something wrong with it." I spend hours puzzling over one piece of sinister evidence which, it is thought, proves that I'm ". . . already manipulating the moral environment so that the forthcoming drama will make sense . . ." And what is it? My interpretation of the law of slander — the 'cornerstone' to this conflict. As follows:

I'd written about the difficulty journalists have in grappling with the law of slander which, I wrote, "prevents the reporter asking a question designed to find out if unsavoury assertions are true." I imagined myself to be sympathetic with the journalist's problem and continued (it's a fascinating detail, this): "a double-edged law which helps the citizen to protect his private life but hampers the journalist in pursuit of a swindler."

After telling me this is a sign that I'm "manipulating the moral environment" my accuser attempts to explain how the law really works. It had taken me a great deal of time to unravel it in the first place, now I'm in even greater confusion. All I can do is simply confess that I don't understand and rebut the accusation of sinister intent. A reply comes back again:

". . . you're going to say I'm patronising. I can't help that if you give the appearance of being stupider than I think you are . . . to labour this, the proposition can read, *either:*
A law which helps the citizen protect his private life, AND hampers the journalist who wishes to expose it

to view, *or:*
A law which helps the swindler to keep his activities
secret, AND hampers the journalist who wants to
expose it. The slander law, in other words, doesn't
have anything to do with the concept of *privacy* as
such, and isn't 'double edged' in the sense you imply."

It's true — I *am* stupid. I stare and stare at the two
propositions. Surely if one can apply "either"
proposition then that makes the law double edged? The
law protects the citizen's private life which is a good
thing but protects the swindler's activity which is a bad
thing — and which is what I'd written originally! I want
to give up, but my accuser returns with further
explanations:

"Put it this way: suppose Lord A has a mistress — a
true fact which he rightly regards as private. Mr B
from the Daily Sneer goes to Lord A's neighbour,
Lady C, who does not know about the mistress, and
says: 'Did you know that your neighbour Lord B
keeps a mistress? Do you think that he ought to be
cut by the County?" There is no way in which the
law of slander would help the unfortunate Lord B
protect his private life, since all defamation law works
on the principle that you can say what the hell you
like about anyone, provided it can be proven true.
(Let's assume that Mr B has a picture of the mistress'
backside with Lord A's fingerprints on it.)
As it happens, the difficulty about slanderous
questions usually arises not with the simple questions
that unpleasant gossip-columnists want to ask about
people's private lives. (Which anyway aren't usually
defamatory: has Belinda Blackstrap got married? Has
Arnold Wesker, the famous playwright, moved from
Highgate to Hampstead?) The difficulty arises when
you are trying to find out whether last year's profit
and loss account contained items that should have
gone into the capital account (i.e. are they fiddling
the profit figures before flogging the business off)

and the like. My objection to your false apposition was, and is, that it suggests that the choice society has to make is between more financial investigation, and therefore more personal prying, or less financial investigation and therefore less prying.

Whether we are going to see eye to eye on this I just don't know. But anyway, I think you must put in either more, or nothing of this."

I have put in more!

There is one curious objection which I cannot understand: a paragraph near the end of *Journey* reads:

"I'm asked if I've found out where the power lies in the newspaper. It's an innocent question which suddenly brings into focus the submerged patterns of fighting egos. I don't envy the Captain who has to control this team of brilliantly intimidating social terrorists."

The objection is strongly felt:

"I dislike your piece chiefly because it calls me a social terrorist (among, by implication, other things). I think that it is (a) untrue and (b) insulting. And I take it seriously because I don't have the faintest sympathy with the sweet English idea that journalism, politics and public affairs generally should be a jovial exchange of custard pies, after which everyone wipes their chops and shakes hands."

It comes as a surprise to me that such a sweet English idea exists but I insist on retaining the description which, when the words "brilliantly intimidating" are added to "social terrorists" and the whole is set in context, is an obviously affectionate one.

But all that's irrelevant. Why, I ask myself, is there such an acrimoniously distorted reading of my long document at all? Why haven't they said: 'Look, you've got some things seriously wrong, let's go through it and see if we can get a more accurate story without interfering with your opinion of us'? Some had done it, even Insight's editor came around to doing it, but . . . not others . . .

Still, keeping my fingers crossed that the acrimony will die down, I rewrite this section the doing of which teaches me about the traps and pitfalls of investigatory journalism into which I've fallen and produces from them some valuable comments on its problems. It only niggles me somewhat that I didn't get all this as a result of perspicacious questioning on my part but had to blunder and evince it in anger. Nevertheless the comments are dramatic and, because deeply felt, sympathetic.

"Your main question is what material would have been denied you if everyone had known that your intention was to publish a piece about The Sunday Times. If the editor had approved that project, I suppose that a number of people would have spoken to you, but probably after first attempting to persuade the editor that there was neither duty nor a merit in opening our doors to any outside writer. If the editor had stuck to his view, then doubtless some people would have cooperated. But in general I think that whatever warmth and expansiveness you managed to generate as a seeker after good lines and good atmosphere for a play would have been much diminished if your purpose had been different . . . I would not have agreed to your coming to any editorial conferences. Even a proper journalist would find it extremely difficult to convey accurately how policy is made at The Sunday Times, or any other paper. I am afraid your own effort quite fails to do it justice . . . But even if you had been able to take a complete tape-recording, and added your interpretative comments, I don't see why I should be in favour of it being published. Is a Cabinet in favour of its meetings being publicised? Is there any reason why a newspaper, if it takes itself seriously, should be any more favourably disposed? If newspapers can get hold of Cabinet minutes or the gist of Cabinet discussions, they will doubtless use them. But that does not mean that Cabinet Ministers have the faintest obligation to surrender these things, if that is not in their interest. Similarly, I can't see that we have the smallest obligation to agree to your publishing our private conversations . . ."

In all fairness it must be added that not everyone agreed:

". . . nothing strikes me as being so offensive/ inaccurate/unacceptable as to rule out publication . . ." and ". . . Naturally I disagree cordially with large portions of it; but I must fight to the death for your right to publish it, damned or otherwise. Actually I enjoyed it very much, though I think you missed several quite important facets of our being (perhaps because we were all so busy making five-layer jokes about them). On balance though I rather deplore the fact that we are not publishing it ourselves . . ." and ". . . For God's sake how embarrassing and wrong that people here should object to what you write, and should make threatening legal noises. That seems to me monstrous, however inaccurate, unfair or damaging they may think your book is. If we do that kind of thing what right have we to go on writing about others? It should be, I think, an absolute principle that we should let others do unto us what we do unto others. Or we should give up altogether . . ."

Finally, Insight's defence of itself:

". . . We not only made no mention of the gynaecologist's personal life, love life, etc., we in fact undertook no enquiries to find out anything about that side of things. Certainly we inquired about her professional record — what did her colleagues etc. think might explain the decision, e.g. was she

Catholic; had she had a gruelling time with abortion requests; any one of a number of things like that which might explain her attitude. Because we found no particularly outstanding personal beliefs, etc., we said nothing about her as a person at all — presenting a very flatly written story simply about the conflict between a child and a doctor; and leaving the reader to side with whoever they wished. That may not be art, and it has its massive limitations. But it certainly is not the sort of brutalising, gutter approach that you credit us with . . . You misunderstood a) the degree to which X was acting and b) the private language 'guilty gynaecologist' . . . It's another example of the shorthand that comes from long proximity that you didn't grasp. (This particular joke relates to a comment from Murray Sayle once: 'There are only two types of story: We Name The Guilty Man. And: Arrow Points To The Defective Part.') Which tells you a lot about popular journalism, and expresses a basic truth . . . This failure to see our work in the round comes out most clearly in your description of the inquiry into bridges. If we described a week's work by listening to the first 15 minutes and then selecting that — plus a few jokes — as representative of the whole, you would be rightly appalled. Yet that is precisely what you have done. Did you know the work we put into that? Did you look at the technical reports we ploughed through, ask what construction experts we had consulted, record any of the long and detailed meetings we held among ourselves and with long-standing technical assistants on this? No . . . Of course, agreed, the power of Insight is frightening, because irresponsible in the real sense of the word.* Hence the almost self-righteous effort to define all the time what one *is* responsible to, what one is trying to do . . . who are we to impinge upon people's lives? (Yet most of the time they are powerful men, not helpless Mrs Jones.)

* Meaning 'power without responsibility'.

What do we hope to find? The truth? But if that is locked away in the private motives, doubts, hesitancies only half recognised even by the principals in any story, how can outsiders hope to understand? . . . But much of your view of the paper — Insight included — was blurred by the difficulties of adjusting stereotypes to reality. Because so many newspapermen really do see themselves in the fast talking, 'Get the story, kid' Ben Hect mould — newspapermen as a breed being in reality insecure and prone to cardigans and commuting, but cherishing dreams of themselves fed mainly by Warner Brothers (*and* don't believe that the Guardian are any different). But newspapers don't really work like that. Only the surface is terribly convincing — so many people want to make it so. The Sunday Times has the added disadvantage, from the outsider's point of view, that the element of parody is perhaps stronger here than elsewhere; yet the surface we do adopt and would call our own — which your editorial conference catches cleverly — is equally phoney . . . There are great limitations to the Insight technique. The Ulster book is a compendium of them, as a perceptive review by Roy Hattersley, the ex-Labour Minister in charge of the Army in Ulster in Wilson's Government, pointed out. The limitations of narrative form as a vehicle for analysis; the limitations of deducing motive from action; the danger that post hoc becomes inevitably propter hoc in a narrative relying upon sequence; the imposition upon a reader, the arrogant demand (unless we are careful) that he trusts us, imposed by the protection of sources; the argument over what we are trying to portray . . . all these are valid problems . . . we don't give a damn whether we emerge 'unblemished heroes and champions of justice', so long as we are at least excoriated for genuine failings . . ."

"Journalism is the task of blaming other people while diverting blame from yourself. That's why good journalists tend to be paranoid."

The leader conferences

"I want to ask John to do something on women being barred from the stock exchange."*

"Quite right. You can't claim to be a fabric of the national economy and then claim the privileges of a private club."

"I was thinking of a light-hearted leader, not an occasion for solemnity."

"Of course not. They're making such fools of themselves."

"They say it's because they wouldn't be able to tell dirty jokes on the floor."

"But John's on the Persian Gulf. Peter?"

"How long is the Persian Gulf?"

"About 300."

"Good, that leaves me about 400 to do the stock exchange."

"Do you want the leader on the Persian Gulf to have a message? A punch line?"

"Yes, start with that joke about the Arabs."

"Which one?"

"Oh, that one about — how does it go? Showing they can't ever agree on anything. Do you have time to do it?"

"Good lor, yes. I'll do it tonight."

"Soyuz? A leader on that?"

"I'd much sooner do Soyuz than the Mafia. I don't believe the Mafia exists."

"What could we do on it?"

* Shortly after this, a ruling was passed to allow women into the Stock Exchange.

"Oh, I thought we could tackle 'what's the point of it all, is it worth it, isn't this a right moment to get together'?"

"By the way, let's get Godfrey to go through all the Pentagon papers and select what he wants and ask what space he wants in an ideal world then tell him it's not an ideal world."

On the one hand they communicate a sense of immediate action, despite the flippant tone, as though the world will, tomorrow, be changed, informed, surprised. It's exciting. Here lies power. And if not action then certainly activity. On the other hand they also communicate the ease and confidence of living in a cocoon. Like actors in a company as opposed to free lance actors. Their fields of responsibility are defined as are the limits to which they need exercise that responsibility. They have a job, known, palpable, for which they have established patterns and precedents every week of the past.

> "I write letters of resignation every year . . . a journalist is only ever a man of the times. Personally, as an academic, I find I'm involved in a great conflict between journalism's demands of superficiality and my own training in academic precision. Sometimes I think I'm in journalism simply because I'm unfit for work."

But a leader conference is considered to be the paper's palpitating heart. There was great concern lest I missed them. I said I'd been to one and was told one was not enough. "You've no idea what heart-searchings go on here over the leaders. We spend hours discussing issues. And the differences of opinion we have! Ha! And the way we reconcile them! We're always having conflicts, changing each other's mind. I'm always changing my mind, I can always be persuaded. Don't believe strength is such a great virtue. Compassion is much more important. That gynaecologist story — you didn't hear the quarrel we had over *that* one . . ."

So, sometime later, I sit in on another leader conference. Only three people present. Mostly there's five or six. Representing university and brilliant youth is a heavy limbed and kindly faced man looking like the brother you've always wanted at your side to be commonsensical, tender and firm. Then, immaculately dressed — thank God! — is the kind of man with age deceptive, charm lethal, and fair good looks reassuring, representing journalism's ambassador to the elegant dining rooms of influence, wit and adequate conversation. And finally, with alertness to danger pouring out of every finely tuned intelligent glance and movement — the captain: a cheeky, thoroughbred working class mongrel about whom I guess that, coming from an underprivileged background, he'd made bloody sure there was no part of the operation he couldn't do himself. (And I shall call them just that: Brother, Ambassador and Captain.)

The Captain begins: "We're rather stuck this week."

The Brother picks up: "Oh I don't know. There's that piece you suggested on the Stockholm conference. All that traffic congestion due to a conference on environment! Nice irony. I'd like to do something on that. Link it up to Peyton's statement. Did you read it? It's quite staggering actually —"

"Yes," says the Captain, "I'm surprised the dailies didn't pick that one up." The Ambassador asks, what.

"Well," continues the Brother, "there's all these hundreds of delegates, all meeting under the United Nations banner, with our own Minister Of Environment, Walker, as one of them; and here's Peyton, a junior minister of transport *under* Walker making this incredible statement in the House about *not* putting certain regulations into force, which had been agreed on in the House last year, remember? Regulations about reducing the noise from cars by three or four decibels?

And why not? Because he'd been under pressure from the car industry who were complaining that it would have forced them into higher costs and reduced their competitiveness in the common market. And Peyton says that as the motor industry is of such importance to the country —"

Captain: "That's just the sort of detail we should be following up. I'm tired of all these end-of-the-world stories when in fact there are hundreds of small problems which *can* be attended to — like the sulphur content of the air."

Brother: "Just what politicians are good at if they're good at anything. Little things like that, cleaning the Thames or the London air, and it works."

Captain: "Oh I'm not complacent about the air of London. They say it'll come back, smog; something to do with the effect of sunlight on the fumes."

The discussion is disjointed. Everyone throwing facts and observations into a common pool from which the shape of the leaders might emerge.

Brother: "I mean look at Rio Tinto Zinc ploughing up North Wales. They found nothing and went off somewhere else. All that promise of work to the local community."

Ambassador: "But if this club of Rome, or whatever it's called, is right and we only have copper for the next 25 years then I should think we ought to plough up the whole of North Wales. After all we're only a small manufacturing country —"

Captain: "*I* should think the answer is to find a substitute for copper."

Ambassador: "Is there one?"

Brother: "And then there's Crossman's argument that it's all very well for you middle class people to start getting upset about pollution and the environment but it all comes from what increases the standards of living of the working class."

Captain: "*Is* that true? Anyone gone into that? Actually worked it out? I mean away with lead in petrol! Away with sulphur in coal! Down with noise!

Fine! But does it really lead to anti-growth?"

The Captain then tells a story of how when he was editor an attack from The Northern Echo on a certain industrial practice by ICI led to ICI modifying some piping system which in turn led to increased demands for lead piping. "*That* wasn't anti-growth, that was stimulation." It's a good story but the Ambassador gently suggests it's a special case and can't really prove a principle.

The early part of the discussion is a kind of 'feeling' session. Tentative. Issues aren't discussed right through, they're dropped and picked up again later. The Captain brings up the railways dispute. Should they do anything on that? It's sniffed at, pawed and passed by. Stockholm engages them more for the moment.

The Captain returns to the Crossman thesis and asks "have we countered it?" Pollution (quality of living) versus wages (material standards of living). "I mean, supposing we said all cars should be kept out of the city centres, would this reduce the need for cars, cut down on production, jobs?" They agree that it's details like that which need to be followed through. "I mean," continues Captain, "there's a brilliant article in The Standard. Anyone read it? About pulling down Soho and what it meant in terms of destroying a community. Absolutely first rate stuff I thought, showing a proper concern for human beings and history and atmosphere. *That's* the kind of approach we should be making. We need to stay off the cosmic level and stick to specifics."

At once my sympathies go soaring. I want to applaud. (And when the paper comes out on the following Sunday there's an article on the Stockholm conference — 'Why the poor always lose' — pursuing the Crossman theme.) But after the initial silent leap of joy the old ambivalence sets in. Why do they merely tinker with such enormous problems? Why do they scatter and dissipate attention instead of focusing it? They seem to be hovering on the edge of something to be grabbed at as a fundamental theme: the Captain's question: what would happen if all city centres were cleared of cars?

Whom would it affect? Not only the car industry's management but also the industry's workers; and from them — the unions; then the pedestrian who might benefit from the increased safety and fresh air; or is it likely that shopkeepers would suffer because less people would come into town? Or would *more* people come? They might, if the public transport system were more effective. And what about free fares during rush hours? And the effects on motor insurance; the decline in revenue from motor tax? And what else? The ageless theme of interdependence. Why didn't they go into it in a big way? Surely such a debate contained many features of those other problems flooding our approach to the year 2000?

I think to myself: if I edited a newspaper I'd make the leader its raison d'etre. If an issue is worth drawing attention to then attention should be drawn to it by onslaught. There are so many questions to ask, so many aspects to consider. Is it seriously considered that an issue is dignified simply by being given a wider column beneath a regal escutcheon? Surely nothing can disguise the little bits of pontification which go thumping down one third of the 'Opinion' page?

A new subject is thrown into the melting pot: the Ambassador thinks the recent bid by France for political leadership of Europe is worthy of a leader. "I mean Pompidou's attitude is a bit like the Trade Unions: 'we'll negotiate providing you come to the table with an already packaged and acceptable offer.' What does 'negotiate' mean? Did you read it this morning? The French want to shift the headquarters for the political secretariat from Brussels to Paris, and they're insisting on French being the official language. It's all obviously a bid for political leadership of Europe and I think we should stand up against it."

The Captain asks if he's against spreading the pleasures of the French language? "Indeed not," says the Ambassador, "as a lover of it myself — no! by all means. But facts are facts, it *is* a minority language and I don't see the sense of spending a lot of money on publicity to promote it."

40

They return to the impending railway strike. "I'm afraid I'm an appeasement man," says the Ambassador. "I mean tell me, someone, one of you who is a 'strength' man, what is hoped will happen by the government remaining firm? Who will it teach a good lesson to, to bring the railway to a halt? Will it establish a principle? And let's forget the precedent of the miners — if that's possible. Is the cost of disruption worth it? Captain, what do you think?"

"I've been trying to work out what I think all bloody week." There's a discussion about the percentages and no one can agree on exactly what is being asked or what is being offered. Is Business News doing anything on it? The editor of Business News is called up (and we'll call him The Business Man).

Now something very strange happens. The Captain says: "Of course, the left feels that the unions must extract all they can get." Someone says "that's anarchy" and someone questions who the hell the left is. There is a pause.

"Trouble is," says the Brother, "the unions used to know what was on and what wasn't on; now they look at a wage packet and ask is it worth striking for anything but a large increase." There's another pause.

Someone says: "And I think there's a tendency to see it as a much larger struggle within competitive society." Pause, yet again, slightly longer.

"The 'them and us' struggle is really on," says the Ambassador. The pause lengthens, like a train of thought grinding to a halt under threat.

Someone says: "And it doesn't help when they can see such enormous profits being made in property." They have paused — utterly.

I sense a profound reflection. Again they seem on the edge of a major debate. Brother touched on it: the actual size of the wage packet. It has always seemed manifest lunacy to me that workers are expected to be happy, civilized, fulfilled and unfearful of the future, doing the work they do for the wages they receive. Today's society is one in which the teacher is scorned

41

as scant investment by bank managers, and the farm worker is planning to ask for a minimum of £25 a week instead of £16.* Planning to — they don't have it yet. What could Captain, Brother, Ambassador, Wesker do with £25 a week? And none of us were super rich, perhaps not rich at all, just comfortable, which meant that we all needed to keep an eye on our bank balances; budgeting was not an alien problem to us. What *are* they discussing? Why don't they simply say that, based on their own experiences of how expensive everything is, average wages are not enough? Why aren't they incredulous at the government's fights to keep wages down? Outraged by that on which a worker is expected to be human and happy.

In that moment of pause — and it is ever so brief — it seems to me that they all see it: the big gulf between the haves and the have-nots, the vision of an impending sharpening of the conflict between 'them and us'; and they remember that all industrial disputes are more than an argument about whether the kitty can be raided for a few pence more or not; they are arguments about the inherent injustices of a competitive, free-for-all system, and a real leader on the railwaymen's demands raises questions of morality and not problems of simple mathematics. They see it, pause, reflect, and — it seems to me — feel impelled to move on.

When Business Man comes in he at once declares his support of the government. "What *I* don't like, and get angry with, are the stories going out, especially our own stories, that the amount offered is miniscule. But *is* it? I mean *I* don't think the government can afford to pay what the unions demand. But, foolishly, they had their ballot, and we encouraged the ballot —"

"*I* was for the ballot," the Captain interrupts. "And I was for the ballot because we all didn't think the men were behind the strike. But we were wrong." Captain's

* The situation has, of course, improved for the teacher (basic minimum £2565), but not for the farm labourer (basic minimum £2028), jumps of just under 150% while the cost of living has jumped 125% approximately from 1971 to 1977.

confession that he and The Sunday Times were behind the ballot because they thought the men were not behind strike action staggers me. Even I could have told them that. Being at the centre of a news machine is obviously no guarantee for correct political evaluations. The Captain, I guess, would be the first to admit that; not even being Marx is a guarantee! But that doesn't seem to be the problem; the problem seems to provoke the question: does being a desk journalist, who is trying to make sense of one problem in the brief time left to him before going on to make sense of another problem, guarantee that you'll *never* make the correct political evaluation?

"What *are* the alternatives?" the Captain chairmanises.

"One: bugger all! Two: get the DP to provide a second Jarrot review. Three: give in and give them their 14% or 16% or whatever it is. I mean we could write a leader that the country just has to put up with the work to rule, or higher fares, or that the entire railways financing and accounts system needs re-organising — which is, incidentally, what *I* really believe to be the answer."

They discuss the miners' break through the wage ceiling. Were they a special case? They all think, yes. Not even they are free from the nation's collective fears of claustrophobia. Our guilts about miners are keenly woven into our childhood myths: miners actually work in those interminable, deep and dungeoned corridors that inhabit ordinary men's nightmares. Give them the money! They might be buried alive under the earth. But railwaymen? They're paid to take joyrides *over* God's earth.

"Right!" says the Captain, "let's have a show of hands. You're in favour of Marsh paying up?"

"Yes," says the Ambassador. "If I'm pushed to the wall, yes, I am. I mean if he doesn't pay up he'll lose so much in fares . . ."

"Well *I* don't believe the government can afford another cave-in," says the Business Man.

"Oh no!" says Ambassador, "Oh I think British

Transport should pay but not at the price of the exchequer, no! Only at the price of the commuter."

"And what," asks Business Man, "if the CBI grit their teeth and say we'll stick to a 5% rise in prices and Marsh has to raise fares *above* 5% to pay for the pay increase?"

"But is it a 5% rise?" the Ambassador asks. "Is that what's needed to cover the wage claim? Does anybody know?"

"I must look into that," says the Captain, and continues: "Is my idea of Jarrot phase-two ridiculous?"

"Trouble is," says the Business Man, "the bulk of all such reports becomes a gloss for the government's failures and the unions throw all the pages into the waste paper basket except the ones referring to their increased wages."

They all consider that perhaps what's needed is simply a guide to the plans — everyone's so confused. No flowery pontifications, just a recapitulation of the possibilities; who's suggesting what; who's saying no; and why.

The Ambassador reminds the Captain that he, the Captain, has the casting vote. "Brother and I are doves, the Business Man here is a hawk, what are you?"

"I'm beginning to feel a bit hawkish on this one," the Captain replies; "in fact I think *I'll* write something on the railways."

"Oh that's a real directive if you like," says the Ambassador.

From which they go on to discuss 'the right of silence', calling in on the Stockholm conference on the way, French intransigence and, finally, deciding to wait till next week to write about the rail dispute. Of the leaders on that Sunday the first points wearily to government hypocrisy over their environment policy, and the second diplomatically spanks President Pompidou's bottom in language faintly reminiscent of astrological forecasts. I can't resist running a Nova prediction for Leo together with the last paragraph of The Sunday Times second leader for June 11th 1972.

"If you intend to make statements from the throne criticising the attitude of your family and near relatives because you feel that you have not of late received the courtesy and respect you deserve, avoid such recriminations around the 16th or you will find yourself — anatomically speaking — out on a limb and with your heart in exile. The new moon on the 20th is in conjunction with the planet Neptune, the influence responsible for so much of the confusion and uncertainty prevalent on the domestic front. Obviously this is the wrong time to take decisions of any consequence affecting the situation in your home. When the sun enters the sign of Sagittarius on the 22nd your optimism and confidence should receive a slight boost, but you would do well to practise a more circumspect and tolerant approach in your personal relationships than is your wont. The new, enlarged EEC will have some vital decisions to take, including agreement on a new Atlantic relationship and on improved relations with Eastern Europe, the Commonwealth and Japan. The autumn summit and the thorough preparations which should precede it, will be an excellent opportunity for a rational and forward-looking discussion of these issues. Instead of indulging in displays of petulance at not having things all their own way, the French will be better employed helping to prepare constructively for the new, interdependent, Europe of the Seventies."

The newsroom

They tell me to be sure and arrive in the newsroom on Saturday. That's when it all happens. I've watched the week start slowly and noted the increased pace as the days passed. Saturday will be the climax. The first, important idea comes to me concerning the play. It must be set like "The Kitchen". All departments on stage at once, the story weaving its way from one group to another; action, movement, dialogue to be continuous, beginning slowly and ending with the hectic activity of the moments just before the pages go down. Perhaps, to the rear of the stage, a large screen of the machines which, as the end approaches, slowly begin to move and spit out the sheets of newsprint with its attendant noise in the background.

It's more difficult to make sense of the long, cluttered newsroom. It's full of new faces behind the desks which through the week had been empty. The 'phone rings non-stop; a secretary singing 'newsdesk' every five minutes punctuates the chatter. A man comes up to me. "They tell me you're Arnold Wesker. Writing a new play about us. Very pleased to meet you, been an admirer for a long time." He, like so many others, provides me with useful and unasked for information. He's a Saturday sub and a weekday official spokesman for the Treasury. "My wife gets the cheque from the Treasury and I come here to earn my beer money." There are three others. One "a Renaissance scholar who writes on obscure poetry by obscure Italian monks. Another who's one of the heads of a BBC overseas news programme. Another who lectures on journalism at the Polytechnic." I sit in a corner, feel a little foolish and exposed, but it's known why I'm here and many are anxious to guide me. "Reporters send in good information badly written; the sub is used to give the story a perspective the reporter has lost. Problem is: the subs, who're so used to badly written stories, often rewrite the good ones also . . . inky-fingered maniacs!"

Snatches of conversation build up what's happening.

"Our copy taker is in chaos and Ian is sitting in his hotel waiting to dictate — can you do something about it? . . . Why doesn't he do the pop festival and then I can do Wimbledon? . . . We're going down to that wedding. It's royalty and the chief feels a little responsible to them or for them or something . . . Ring him up, tell him copy is OK but ask him what he means by the top of page 7 where it says 'the

secret transcripts have been released!' What
transcripts have been released, by whom, to whom
and about what? . . . Right! Rand on the front page
and Pakistan on the newspage. Rand is surprised
Elsberg could leak so much. We'll believe them . . .
We'll put Wilson here, abortion over here, Hanratty
down there and that'll leave the upper right space for
the photo of Solti . . ."

I ask: "Can anyone tell me why they're giving front
page space to a photo of a fifty year old opera
conductor holding his fourteen month old baby?" The
reply is: "Well, we've got a story about a fourteen year
old hanging, one about a mother urging her daughter to
death in order to save her from the shame of producing
a bastard, a story about the Common Market which
we're all agreed is a turn-off subject by now, so, with a
gruesome front page like that you need a drop of human
warmth to make our millions of readers like the world
just a little bit on their Sunday off work. Right? Next
problem."

I pick up spare sheets and try to read with the new
eyes I've been given these past days, but it's no good. I
still can't get beyond the first paragraphs of most
articles. A treacherous thought brings me down: newspapers are not boring so much as they induce a sense of
futility. After the first sentences I think: what the hell!
The language is predictable, the facts likely to be
inaccurate and contradicted in another newspaper, or if
not inaccurate then specially selected or incomplete,
or the situation will change tomorrow or something
else is more important or there's just too damn much of
it anyway. I'm simply reading what someone has been
interested in for the space of a couple of hours spent
interviewing and typing. I'm being agitated by a week of
someone else's enthusiasm, tossed about by ephemeral
curiosities, whipped up by typewriter emotions. "The
essence of good journalism," says someone, "is to
remain bored until the opportune moment." I feel
dangled on the end of strings, manipulated.

But this day has its special excitement. The front page is being newly designed. The left hand column is to be extra wide to take a new idea, a kind of 'stop-press' selection of late news items. The head printer is in a panic. I'm not sure if I understand the problem but it's to do with the new column being wider than on the continuation over-sheet. Someone gets irritated. "Tell him the British have just sent a man to the moon but we're ignoring it because it'll upset the layout of the front page." The front page is drawn out again and again. Messengers stand around waiting to be given bundles of papers: "Business News, please." "Sports desk, please." "Foreign." "Processing, please." The paper is slowly built up, the various editors hovering around a main table where the head layout man draws and re-draws the placement of articles with his ruler. Changes reflect the editors' ideas of which issues are more important than others. The headlines of other papers are scanned, their scoops can alter an entire week of planning. It's a creative process.

Part Two

"They've lived so long in a world of expenses, first class hotels and travel and they can't remember what it's like to live any other life. I've got old aunts and uncles and friends of parents. I still know. Not them. That's what's fresh about the underground press, for all its faults. They don't send people from the outside, in. They're in already. In the prison, in the dole queue, in the slum house, in the demonstration."

The machines

It's insisted that I visit the noisy deep of the building in time to watch the printing machines turn out the first edition. It's vast, thunderous and impressive. There are nine beauties each capable of turning out 200,000 papers. Installed over a period of about six years from 1962 they cost approximately £7 million. Before completion they already looked out of date compared with the newest equipment. And the management is now confronted with having to employ about 2,000 throughout when, I'm informed, the paper could be produced with a third fewer people.

"The printing machinery is Victorian. I mean consider — we type out our copy, sub-editors knock it into shape, compositors type it out again on the lino-type machine which produces proofs needing proofing. When the proofing's approved then the lino type of each page is assembled into a metal frame called a forme, copy sheets are hand-pressed from this and proofed again. Then the forme is put into a large mangle operation where a soft flabby cardboard is subjected to considerable pressure to produce a mirror image of the sheet and by this time it's become something called a flong which another

machine flings into a half cylindrical shape of lead.
Two half cylinders make one side of a double sheet
so they have to be bolted to the rotary presses into
one end of which you feed a large roll of paper.
Barrels of ink are drained into the machines and
knobs are guarded to ensure the correct flow and
pressure and, when all this is ready, you press a
button which ends you up with a neatly cut and
folded Sunday Times. All this instead of using
photographic or web-offset techniques with
computerised methods of cutting and folding. Why
don't we switch? Because it reduces manpower and
the unions are protecting the livelihoods of their men.
To start a newspaper from scratch you used to need
£10 million, today you can do it for £100,000. The
implications are tremendous; instead of newspapers
being only open to a handful of millionaires it's now
possible for you and me to start a paper and the
operation could be handled by a girl who'd done a
typing course instead of men who'd had to serve a
five year apprenticeship. Typists earn £20 a week,
printing craftsmen £60. Who can blame the unions?
And they have a very strong weapon, I can remember
two occasions on which agreements were signed,
sealed and delivered but on the Friday night they
changed their mind and asked for more so we had a
pistol at our head. You can't *not* put out newspapers.
They know, you see, that it's a declining industry.
Sooner or later, they say, we're going to get screwed
so we'll make all we can as fast as we can which
results in the screw being applied sooner."

Four things strike me: the noise, the vastness of the
operation, the men with withered hands, and the dull,
slick smartness of the production managers who seem
tough, shrewd and idle. Another treacherous thought
brings me down: the arguments demanding just return
for the worker's labour have gradually, over the years,
also become a false argument glorifying that labour and,
here's the treachery, the glorification has grown

commensurate with our own thanksgiving for not having to do the soul-destroying jobs ourselves. If we are seen to be defending his rights then the working man is disarmed from complaining of the boredom and humiliation of his work. The more we endow his work with intelligence the less guilty we feel for the satisfactions of our own professions. Deafened by the noise of the machine room I understand that the factors to be considered in a wage claim are not only the rising cost of living or the correct figure for the type of product, or the degree of responsibility or apprenticeship involved but a new factor which could be named 'the undesirability factor'. The less attractive the job the more must be paid for engaging him in it. And the more our society confronts a man with the glamours and pleasures of other worlds the more they are going to have to pay the man whose own world they've made appear less attractive to him. Looking at the men in the machine rooms who retain an incredible cheerfulness, humour and natural intelligence I find myself thinking not 'how admirable and noble' but 'thank God it's them and not me' and I'm relieved to move out of the noise into the comparative peace of a Saturday upstairs.

> "The journalist is a kind of actor, he makes his decisions only under pressure, when 'the world' is waiting for the story; hence his reluctance to *talk* about a story, because if it's aired, it evaporates."

The arts pages

"We keep ourselves to ourselves, here." As a literary man I should feel at home in this office. I think I am. At any rate I make a greater success of the pretence that I am. Mild resentments that my book of lectures received scant attention from these arbiters of taste crumble when I discover they receive over 9,000 books a year, the rate increasing yearly, of which they manage to review a fifth. "What chance the new novels?" I ask. They tell me they're aware of the problem of new novels and give them special attention. "But we make mistakes and regret certain books we've passed up." I look through the shelves. Crisp, fresh things; books demand to be possessed. What happens to the review copies? "We pack off batches to reviewers whose field they are, they decide what to review then keep or sell or give them away. Sometimes people stroll through and take books — we have a critic who's a Japophile with a passion for butterflies, flower arrangements and stone gardens. The rest? They get sold and the money goes into the Thomson account."

Critics clutter in and out to check their copy, pick up new books, confirm theatre or travel arrangements, complain and gossip. Faces are at last attached to names I've seen each week at the top of a review column: Felix Aprahamian, Cyril Connolly, Julian Symons. One critic asks: "Wouldn't it be better if someone else reviewed this book? I find his writing so awful that I'm beginning to feel it's unfair." Harold Hobson rings in and I whisper: "Tell him his favourite playwright sends regards," thinking he'll say something like "what's Harold Pinter doing in your office?" But he guesses who it is and we chat, completely ignoring the massive attack I'd written on critics some weeks before. What do I expect? That we should snarl, churlishly ignore one another? It's not easy to be rude and courtesy doesn't prevent me from attacking nor, incidentally, protect me from being attacked.* I don't feel the need to be aggressive to prove where I stand. Nevertheless I'm beginning to feel a little like the journalist who once came to interview me for an article he was writing for Private Eye on Centre 42 and

* Hobson never did acknowledge my article on critics — *Casual Condemnations* — published in Theatre Quarterly (Vol 1, No 2, 1971), but bided his time till a new play came up for review a year later — *The Old Ones* — then he leapt!

the Roundhouse. He regretted coming, he said, because the hard edge of his critical faculty was blunted by my 'charm' which, even so, didn't prevent him making fourteen errors of fact in that truth-at-all-costs public school powder keg.

As arts editors they find especial pleasure feeding me information and stories from behind their three desks which, bumper to bumper brings them daily face to face with each other.

"Everyone, except us, has to be careful of the Irish edition, Catholic sensibilities, certain omissions for them or copies might be impounded ... Do you know that the first edition of most Sunday newspapers is read by competitors at six o'clock on the Saturday evening to see if there's a scoop they've missed which they can then get into their later editions? The really big scoops are not put into the early editions at all, Philby in Moscow for example ... It was at a concert of a Beethoven symphony and Carl Orf's Carmina Burana, and our music critic overheard one of the members of the orchestra say, in a loud voice 'now that we've buggered up Beethoven we'd better fuck Orf' ... He's not rude, just mannerless ... Yes, he writes his reviews by hand, sends them in unpunctuated and when we've knocked them into shape he collects them to store and sell to the university of Texas ... The better they are the less they mind your criticism of their reviews, it's only the minor critics who go in for tantrums ... The rumour is that he puts deliberate mistakes into his columns in order to attract readers letters which then provides copy for his next week's column; gets annoyed when the subs correct his galleys ... He sort of got the money for his soul without actually selling it ... He had a passion, though not now that he has children of his own, for the most exotic mammals ... We all take notice of colleagues, look for praise from each other, I can still be affected and placed in seventh heaven if the editor passes me

54

*and says 'that was a good piece you wrote last
week'..."*

I glance at the mail lying around on desks. Every
morning the secretary goes through the ritual of opening
fifty or so letters deciding who needs to answer which. I
ask if all letters are answered. They are, often by hand.
Can I see one? I'm told I can read whatever I like. Many
make me blush, they read like those early, pompous
letters to editors one used to write as an adolescent.

"Whatever your decision it's bound to prove
expensive. If you reject it, you will discover very
soon, as I have already warned you, that you have
missed 'the scoop of the century'. If you accept it
and publish the articles I shall expect payment at a
rate that will enable me to complete my life's work
during the next two or three years."

The replies are patient and courteous. And poems?
"Oh yes, we receive those all right. World disasters bring
them in. And Prince Philip's birthday. Says much for
the poetic soul of the British public but hardly contri-
butes to British poetry I feel."

The traffic of people is continuous. It seems incredible
to me that such a packed and carefully constructed
newspaper is ever produced. No one seems to work,
they only ever appear to be reading newspapers. In the
corridor on the way to the lavatory one of the Insight
team stops me. They'd all been affected by my week in
their office. "I was over-reacting like hell, trying to be
too casual; and every time we lifted the 'phone you'd
reach for a pen and immediately we all felt we were
talking gibberish. As for the editorial conferences I hear
they were hamming it up all the time. Everyone playing
professional journalist."

The lavatory paper in Thomson House is of the old
fashioned kind: hard, glossy on one side. It tears at
one's tender corners and blocks up the pot; though it's
true soft packs do run the risk of dirtying one's hands!

On the way back from the toilet a columnist stops me and confesses he occasionally puts trivial items in his column to retain contact with that same person concerning whom a future story is looming up. Meanwhile in the office, a book reviewer who is also a novelist and film-script writer comes in to collect his book for the week and check his proofs: "Is it your idea of a joke, a correction or an improvement to change my words from 'to put it mildly' to 'to put it wildly'?" They begin to reminisce over past misprints and another is produced sounding like something from Joyce's *Tales of Shem and Shaun*: 'They become incredibly wound up; yet there is method in their madness for the unwinding is ceremonious and without a bitch.'

My presence makes it irresistible for the book reviewer to air dark grievances. He suggests that writing novels is more difficult than writing plays; I leave it to others to argue that one out. Then his real complaint emerges: new plays command greater attention than new novels, a first night is treated as more of an event than publication day. I'm so eager to concede he's right that I forget to remind him he trafficks in the ballyhoo of films. But, just as I'm really enjoying being out and about and thinking how pleasant it is to exchange ideas with fellow writers, his real complaint blossoms into a personal grudge. "I mean," he says, "one does get a bit tired of hearing about 'our Arnold' . . ." Stay at home, Wesker, any hour can be the hour of the assassin.

> "A journalist is a man who possesses himself of a fantasy and lures the truth towards it."

I ask about relationships with the outside world. Do literary editors have fraught relationships with publishers and writers? Aren't they anxious about the parties and lunches to which they're invited? Haven't they got a nervous twitch, confronted with sweetness from interested persons? Do they ever know when they're liked for their own sakes? What about my presence? No! No! They love having me around, didn't I want a job? Wouldn't I like to review for them? Delighted to have someone from the outside with comments, suggestions, new conversation; and of course they're worried about being manipulated but what can they do? They listen to those whom they trust and respect, decline when their own instincts are strong, pick winners, losers, have regrets, victories, quarrels with themselves and each other. What can ever be satisfactory in such an unsatisfactory world? They discourage sneers in their reviewers and cover as much as they can without too much loss of seriousness. But they have as many pages as the paper's advertising will allow and advertising is sometimes scarce.

I am to hear this again and again. The big debate between whether a newspaper should depend upon advertising or the sale price for its existence. Three months after decimalisation The Sunday Times used the change to creep up from 1/3 to 1/7 (8p), a leap of 27%. Some say it should have gone up to 10p at once, others that it should be 12p, a price increase of 100%. "If we aim for 50% advertising and 50% from the price of the paper, rather than one third to two thirds as it now is, we might lose the low income readers but then that would boost the confidence of the advertisers in the readership and it would pay off that way." (Oh? Do we not want nasty, low income readers for such a serious paper? Is seriousness only for those who can afford it?) Everyone complains they're not given enough space and advertising gets the blame.

The jostling for room is fierce and involves proclaiming the greater importance of one's own piece over one's colleagues'. The most aggressive journalists are the youngest: arrogant and left wing; though The Sunday Times still has old fashioned veins enough to dilute even their hot blood. It's a journal with bits and pieces of socialists floating around like flotsam "after the havoc caused by their rise into affluence". However, guilts make them fight harder for their good causes and hustle brusquely for their space. The older and cannier ones have other methods. "The thing to do is try and get a foothold at the top of the next page and press down. It's more difficult to press up."

I ask, why not allow critics to review the plays they like and merely mention those they despise, and if that means there's only 100 words in the theatre column one week, so what? The reply is that people opening their Sunday papers look forward to reading a critic's piece and would be disappointed to miss it even though it were a disinterested bumbling on. And as for the critic himself! What? Him give up his precious space?

My next question commands immediate respect; how much does a journalist give himself to his paper. Ah! there you have it. Sooner or later everyone is forced to make the decision between family and newspaper, between public dedication and private responsibility, between wearying battles for power and demeaning squabbles of wedlock. There is the odd reporter who begs to be sent abroad to avoid his wife or family, others develop mild (some not so mild) schizophrenia. "What I want to do is slide around having little conversations, but I can't quite give up the glamour of catching a plane and having access to important people." Most simply become tired.

"And one grows old, you've no idea, at 32 one is old already . . . You really feel it when you've got deputies under you; being people's deputies is an invitation to an assassination; if you do you create a bad atmosphere, so I didn't. But now I've got a deputy under me I have to work out what my attitude is. Do I encourage him, push him? I do, but I wonder. Credit grabbing is one of the sicknesses of the profession, it takes it out of you . . . You can tell he plays the power game because he's so bad at it, frustrating really, wasteful . . . When Kruschev was sacked, this reporter, one of our top men, tried to

*'phone through to the Kremlin. Didn't stop to think
that neither of them would be able to speak the
other's language, just automatically reached for the
'phone. The spark goes. Last night on TV I was
watching the awful tragedy of the three Russian
astronauts dying in space and I was thinking — yes,
now how can we handle that? This way? Yes, maybe.
That way? Yes, well — I'll sleep on it. Years ago I'd
have immediately rung up people and started
generating ideas . . . If you're young and in charge
and you want to deflate an older journalist my advice
to you is: when he brings his piece you flip through it
and then throw it on the desk and say 'well, honestly,
I didn't expect you to show me something like this'.
. . . If you invade people's private lives it swarms over
the organisation of your life . . . We were out to get
him and then he went out to get us, it all grew very
ugly and vicious and ended up in a personal vendetta.
I wanted to get all I could on the man to hang, knife
and destroy him utterly and he attempted to do the
same to us, ringing up our wives and telling them to
get their husbands to lay off or else . . ."*

"That's what a journalist sees as his
function: naming the guilty men — his
yardstick is one of unswerving idealism."

Another editorial conference

The editor has a knack of ignoring sour remarks and the
undercurrent tensions which betray themselves through
the odd, demolishing comment: "Yes, it's a nice quiet
piece." He employs a candour which sets him among his
colleagues rather than a patronising tolerance which
would place him outside them. Someone tells me this
story about him: "I was sitting in the editor's office

with the editor's two secretaries watching tennis on his TV set when he walks in with a fellow director. He steps back, embarrassed to have intruded. 'Sorry,' he says, 'I'll go somewhere else.' " At this conference he wears a maroon shirt and silver tie which reminds me of a 1920's Chicago mobster. The conference begins.

"What's happening on the Dimbleby TV programme? I thought it was very good actually. But then I've changed my mind six times on it already so I'm not a very reliable witness."

"There's a letter for you in our pigeonhole from a Pakistan official saying how disappointed he is that such a distinguished newspaper could lower itself, etc., etc., and he's cutting his subscription."

"I think we ought to have a very good reporter in India in case something blows up between her and Pakistan. It's a fascinating situation — no, I mean really, we ought to be there, in case war breaks out."

Someone raises their hand. "Me, please. But I think the Naxalite situation is even more important, more than anyone thinks."

"What about the fishermen of England and the Common Market?"

"You and Peter look into the fishermen will you? By the way, what about our new news digest on the front page, any comments?"

"I don't quite know what the journalistic theory is."

"Well, it's a service. It's also a good design breakthrough. Our front page is less old-fashioned now."

"Our middle pages are still full of old-fashioned layout, though."

"Yes, and I think we ought to take a look at those too, get to look more like the magazine."

"Problem is, our layout is still dictated by old advertising agency agreements which keep us stuck to the old column widths."

"That article on convenience foods, is it a big story or not?"

"I thought we were going to find out *if* they are being sold bullshit."

"If they're not being sold bullshit, it's not a good story."

"I'm very bored with the issue of shelling peas."

So, the situation in India is 'fascinating' is it. War might break out! What else do I expect? That they should maintain a sombre or thunderous manner at all times? I train myself to catch the inverted commas they place around their statements. Everyone is terrified of making a fool of himself. No opinion or suggestion can be proffered too sonorously. Sentiment and passion must be reserved for the story itself. Among themselves they must appear controlled, aloof, disengaged. I subdue offended sensibilities and try to be 'mature' about it. If war breaks out there *should* be a good reporter there. The *prevention* of the war is something to be attended to elsewhere, by other means. The doctor doesn't weep while contemplating what the diagnosis is, nor even when he plunges in the scalpel that may heal.

> "People sitting around in offices, lost, that's all a newspaper is, sitting around waiting for ideas to come, wondering what the hell to do next."

Look!

Look!'s office contains wasted women. "It isn't the most scintillating week's work is it? All that effort and we have a column dealing with birds, male sterilisation and the men who make suits for £130 each." Women are always more impressive than men; they seem to intuit truths and real motivation. Much more compelling than the dreary brilliance of men who are simply 'well informed'. "We should be provocative as well as practical. 'Down with children', 'must mothers of handicapped children be martyrs?' — that sort of thing

. . . and we should be more visual, forced to look for the more potent image than the brilliant phrase. I love being stretched. After all, we earn a good wage and I feel I ought to deserve it . . ."

A young man brings in a canvas chair; simple, wooden deal struts, screwed into shape, the canvas glued and tacked. It's low slung, unvarnished and cheap. He's asked to leave it with them for a few days. If they decide it's good value for money they'll promote its virtues, saying where it can be bought and for how much; but nothing will indicate it's an advert and a percentage of the sales will go to The Sunday Times. The information surprises me. Don't I remember that if a group of M.P.s take space to argue an issue they must pay for it and the print will be boxed in saying 'this is an advertisement' to prevent it being confused with editorial copy?

A letter from a reader creates interest and the promise of a story. She writes saying she knows a family — 'a lovely little family' — with two children, where the husband was refused a sterilisation operation on the National Health and had to pay £30 to get it done privately. Hands are rubbed, it seems their other article on male sterilisation has started something, miniature battle stations are called; they'll do something more about this one in view of the problems of population explosion. Look! is very concerned about too many people in the world eating up resources. But, coincidentally, I happen to glance through their book of back numbers and find that, on August 30th 1970, there was an article on the negligees created by a beautiful black designer, Rose Lewis of Knightsbridge, who herself was seductively modelling one of her creations. She is quoted, with that obvious delight the English take in their unserious, unpretentious, light-hearted view of this sad, old world, as saying: "I'm proud to have played my part in the population explosion and I feel responsible for early wedded bliss in many marriages."

"I feel that our role is to slightly balance the serious, if not ponderous, side of the paper by articles which are, yes, slightly titillating." "Sexually titillating?" I ask. "Yes." It worries me that they use the word titillating and I press them again: is that what they really mean? "After all," I say, "the word means 'cheap thrills'." They retract; no, that's not what they mean. Such loose use of words desperately trying to make the world seem a gayer place appears to produce a philosophy of light-heartedness which is not only sloppy but sometimes dishonest. As a result of a series about a fat girl getting into attractive clothes, and feeling not exactly happy but at least unanguished about her size, many letters came in asking how she did it. The letters caused some embarrassment because on investigation it was found that some of the photographs didn't show her back where gaping holes betrayed that the dresses could not be done up. This story is not relished either as a boast or a confession but emphasises the sense they feel of trivial pursuits. "We're supposed to be good at gossip and writing about boys and knickers. You have to be Mary McCarthy or mistress of an editor to be sent to Vietnam. Even Mary McCarthy had to pay for herself." Neither is their pretence of 'unseriousness' always echoed in their columns. Tucked between the 'knickers and boys' stories are occasional anonymous pieces, like the articles by a woman about her depressed husband, a stark and moving account reflecting the heart of many relationships, worthy of the opening paragraphs of a good novel.

As with every group I encounter they arm me with anecdotes.

"Seventeen of us from The Sunday Times once wrote different chapters of a book called 'I Knew Daisy Smutten?' and the publisher held a party for us at his house. Thought us very low indeed he did. And when, after a power cut which brought complete darkness to the party, the lights came back on again, he was caught clutching two priceless pieces of sculpture to his chest . . . And so Shelley Winters says to this reporter 'Vittorio Gassman and I were just mad about

*each other physically and couldn't keep our hands off
each other if we were in the same room. Then he
learned to speak English and I learned Italian and we
found we hadn't a thing in common' . . . We have a
very strange house nurse on The Sunday Times. One
girl went up to her and asked her for something
stronger than aspirin as she'd had a series of
continuous headaches. 'Oh,' said the nurse, 'you've
probably got a tumour on the brain!' . . . What do we
do with all these books we receive? Oh, wait till they
accumulate then sell them and occasionally indulge in
rounds of champagne . . . a prawn omelette was his
idea of an exotic night out . . . Can't move a cabinet
or a chair or even change a plug on your own; must
call the men from downstairs or there'd be a strike
. . ."*

Printing error in Look! 28th February 1971: Headline:
"Controlling Sex — by Lord Fisher. This is an extract
from the former Archbishop of Canterbury's new book,
Control of Sex, to be published Friday at £1.75 . . ."

Apology in the following week's edition: "Lord
Fisher's book from which Look! extracted a chapter
last week is called *Touching on Christian Faith* and will
be published . . ."

Look! blames the agent.

One issue produces an interview with a famous
playwright and his wife about their clothes. It seems out
of character and I ask how the interview was conducted.
Was it a wide-ranging discussion over many subjects out
of which the interviewer extracted choice quotes?
Someone tells me 'no', the couple were told it would
only be about their clothes and that that was how they
actually spoke. Did I think it made them look ridiculous?
Hoping it doesn't sound offensive I say 'yes'. Then
comes the shock: so did they.

"But don't you feel they ought to have been warned?"
I ask.

"No, they've been in the game a long time, they
know what words appear like in print. The piece wasn't
a distortion."

"Not a distortion of those one and a half hours," I say, "but those one and a half hours may distort the whole picture of their lives."

"Oh, I don't know, it's only a portion."

"But do you believe every portion, every wart needs to be magnified? Is that the price to be paid for being allowed to be a writer?"

"People in public life know what they're exposed to." Someone observes that I'm asking serious questions about a flip piece and I feel foolish at disturbing a kind of cult of frivolity. Poor artist! While attempting to be a 'man of the world', thinking that's the way the world is: publicity at any price, he's lured into making such a fool of himself.

One lunch time there's an 'ideas conference'. French bread, cheese, a bottle of red wine and a thick strawberry and cream laden cake baked by my wife for the occasion. They toy with the idea of a series on people's obsessions; another on 'my best friend'. Who should start it? I suggest Bernard Levin. The unseriousness of the English coupled with the 'inverted comma' tone of newspaper chat is very intimidating but I risk offering them an idea for a series: 'the morality of fashion'. I quote them Ruskin: "But whatever happens to you, this, at least, is certain, that the whole of your life will have been spent in corrupting public taste and encouraging public extravagance. Every preference you have won by gaudiness must have been based on the purchaser's vanity; every demand you have created by novelty has fostered in the consumer a habit of discontent; and when you retire into inactive life, you may, as a subject of consolation for your declining years, reflect that precisely according to the extent of your past operations, your life has been successful in retarding the arts, tarnishing the virtues, and confusing the manners of your country!" I must have been mad.

Part Three

"I'm in it to get rid of all my phobias and hang-ups, to have a go at them. It's all entertainment isn't it? You can't underestimate the man in the street, he makes up his own mind, doesn't he? Doesn't believe any of it. And I'm aiming at all those middle class fascists anyway. It's all a joke. They love it. Feel honoured to be attacked."

Bi-annual pep talk

A hundred people sit in the director's dining room trying to appear at ease. Not everything I hear can be repeated, but some? Surely! I can't resist it.

"No big declarations. Circulation gone up fantastically, even with the price rise, and it's the biggest rise in the history of this paper and certainly in Fleet Street . . . what a terrific success story that is . . . and with the Sunday newspaper market contracting . . . our problem is that like everyone else we're dependent on the British economy. Recession, slump? Then no advertising . . . but don't get depressed . . . we're editorially very strong. I'm grateful for all the scoops. I don't know how we do it week after week. Personally I think we could have got away with a price rise of 10p let alone 8p. I believe in a high priced newspaper, we can't depend on advertising forever . . . Some things have been helpful . . . If you take everything in the last budget: corporation tax, S.E.T., profits tax, the lot, it all used to be no good to the company. Such improvements don't, of course, alter our editorial policy towards the government . . ."

Someone asks, referring to some figures mentioned, "what do they mean in percentages?"

Answer: "I don't think I've worked out percentages. You've got to give me notice of a question like that."

Questioner: "I didn't have notice of your speech."

Everyone pretends not to take the gathering's

purpose seriously, but a child-like delight is in their eyes to be told they'd done so well. They feel sheepish these grown, powerful, opinion-making men and women, sitting together, being reminded of school days again. And suddenly it occurs to me, as I look at them, that the attractive quality of the journalist is the aura of other people's power which he carries around with him. He functions in excitements other people create. Now, as I watch them, huddled together and stripped of their individual columns, made one — and vulnerable — by their common attentiveness to the dear Captain's words, I can see it. And that pirated aura gives their opinions an intimidating but borrowed aggressiveness while relieving them of action and the responsibility of action; the existence of Captains always speaks of relieved responsibilities.

> "They play this great game at work and then they shuffle home on the commuter train to suburbia. They need this fantasy world to compensate for their lives."

Half time

My third week comes to an end and I feel it's time to try and organise some preliminary thoughts. Is there a journalistic mind? Does it only come alive with the smell of blood? Is contact with men and women who are giants in their field a sad and inevitable enticement to lilliputian attitudes.? "The demeaning sneers of routine journalistic accounts," is a phrase Nick Tomalin uses in the book on Crowhurst. But journalism involves more than routine accounts. I'm told journalists become cross when academics refer to their work as 'instant history'. On the other hand someone confessed he was terrified by notions of 'considered and responsible journalism'. Facts need to be known but because it's recognised that fact is not truth therefore interpretation is attempted. Opinions are offered. The function is valid

69

but what factors prevent the honest performance of the function? Has anyone named them? Have guards been erected against them? Literature can touch truth because the writer measures and relates facts to his own imperfections in order to arrive at understanding. Few journalists dare measure what they write alongside their own private behaviour, hence so much maudlin sympathy, no real pity, and all idealism is suspected of being pretentious. "The real resentment against 'do-gooders' is that they're so impractical. So you try to shoot them down and then you realise you're a big wolf with a stick knocking at a fly and then you get a conscience and feel you want to help them." There's confusion and often tortured self-searching. "There's the archangel and the cynic in all of us; the archangel embarrasses and produces the cynic." The flow between offices is significant. It's a movement of people sniffing each other out, cuddling up for warmth and reassurance. Ideas are tested on colleagues. Producing a newspaper finally necessitates, despite the quarrels, working together in a close cooperation which produces a bonhomie, loyalties, a sense of purpose and even – yes, though they might shudder — brotherhood; and this creates the illusion that something 'brotherly' is being done. Accuse the journalist of being a snide, hunting, destructive animal and he will flinch, be hurt and surprised, because he can only remember the excitement of having worked together with brilliant colleagues and chummy good-old-working-class-printing-men. He can only recall the infectious enthusiasm of sharing 'hot history', the satisfying weariness of staying up late to get the story right, the friendships that remain after the battles over space and story priorities. All that sweet, shared endeavour leads them to forget that what the endeavour produces may not itself be sweet.

Contempt is difficult for them to conceal. They've met everybody, talked with all sorts, and are themselves terrified of being quoted on anything.

"The thing is they aren't giving out prepared speeches

so they can't remember what they said, in this way you can always improve on what they said and make it appear as if they've spoken in good English . . . One of the lessons of the Maxwell case is that you should never go overboard in praise of any business man, always play it safe and leave openings for yourself . . . My contempt for the Western European business man is increasingly extending to the whole spectrum of human beings . . . There is no trade unionist who I cannot buy with an overload of food or drink or money, my expenses are the highest in Thomson House because it costs so much to bribe trade union officials . . . I find most people so boring in what they say that my slow long-hand is fast enough to catch what's worthwhile . . . Weinstock is one of the most intelligent men we've met who is more intelligent than us, and we don't meet many of them . . ."

Perhaps it's for this reason that, though he cares, the journalist only feels comfortable (or safe?) in the destructive tone of voice. You rarely find a journalist celebrating except in the Business News where certain makers of money impress by their forceful handling of men or the rise of their profits dividend. It wouldn't occur to them to admire the civilised failure, not in print anyway — but more of them later. Nor is the sad, but heartily brave, tone of self-contempt missing either.

"I believe in the capitalist system so I have no conflicts. Conflicts? Hah! I've been looking for them for years; always wanted to be able to resign on a matter of principle . . . Professional standards? I don't believe journalists have a profession, I don't know what that profession is anyway, and certainly they don't have standards. It's the law of the jungle and not a very colourful one . . . No one should take any notice of attacks from Private Eye. The best people don't. I mean most people are proud to be there. You only find journalists suing, they're the first to reach for their solicitor . . . It's like being in a pub and as

long as your wallet is full any number can play and
you know at the end of the day no one can question
your motives, you can't be done for it. As little as
you have the right to do it so no one has the right to
judge or stop you . . . And when there's a drive to cut
expenses in all departments everyone makes their
moral pitch to defend their fraudulent demands . . .
Then after a while one gets sick of hotels and the
quick friendships with people about whom one has
finally to write something unsympathetic . . . I mean
if you go to Ulster and look at the journalists there,
sitting around in pubs, drunk, and a bomb goes off in
the Falls Road so they draw lots who should go and
bring the story back for all of them; it's screwy. Tell
you what, the best reporter in Ulster is the barman.
He tells them there's an explosion and they all rush to
their 'phones. And these are the men upon whom the
world relies for its information."

"When I'm in a tight corner, worried
about a hole in my space, I know there's
a pile of Wall Street Journals sitting
there and I can always rely on them to
provide me with a story — that and the
Essex Recorder. Of course that's how all
overseas journalists work, they read the
local newspapers and send back precis
reports."

Business News

When I ask can I sit around in their large office for a
week or so I'm told that of course, I'm welcome. Why,
they were even beginning "to feel neglected and feared
you'd bypass us. We were told 'Wesker won't visit you,
you're the heart of the capitalist society he despises'."
Can journalists really operate only with such simplified

images? Someone has assured me in a previous week: "The greatest thing about Business News is that they tend to deal with finance as theatre." And sure enough, on my first day, I'm greeted by a strikingly dramatic and breathless voice (whose breathlessness is due to the fact that it's sardonically laughing at what it's saying at the same time as it's saying it): "We've been told, ha ha, by the Telegraph, ha ha ha, that we're like the, ha, TV power game programmes, ha ha ha, tending to see all business as a jungle and all business men as nasty, ha, wrangling, ha, sly, ha, grinning, ha, smooth handshaking, ha, and backstabbing villains . . ." I become anxious as to whether he'll make it to the end of the sentence. He does. The anxiety is worth it. Far from them being pillars of capitalist society they seem to me an army of very bright urban saboteurs. "You see, it's a question of the credibility of The Sunday Times which, as an old conservative family newspaper, commands more respect than, say, The Observer, which is known for its liberal policies, and therefore we're a better journal through which to infiltrate radical views — more people will believe us." The sardonic spirit pervades each one of them.

Or, almost each one. "I believe Arnold Weinstock was successful because he started at the top." This promises to be interesting — Mr Weinstock* is about to become the personality of my week with them. "The great thing about him is he's so sane. 'The man's no good?' he asks. 'Can he go now? Before five o'clock? Why wait?' And indeed, why wait?" I deem it wise not to answer. Good journalists must record. "If he has to sack 5,000 men because of waste he'll do it. Why not? And he'll justify it by saying it's better for the sacked ones because men get depressed hanging around doing nothing, they lose their self-respect." Ah yes, I say to myself, that'll catch in your throat, men losing their self-respect for not being given machines to mind. Compassionate man, Weinstock. "And those that stay know that they're

---

* Now Lord Weinstock.

good because Weinstock has kept them and so they're men of confidence, they work harder." A Solomon, no less. But, I'm foolish and ponder 'Solomon's' motives. Greed? My earnest companion disabuses me. "Waste! Waste offends him, makes no sense. It's only incidentally that his policy produces more profits — and don't raise a wry eyebrow at that." I try not to raise a wry eyebrow at that. It's easy; everyone is so friendly and honest.

In fact, as I write this piece, I make the discovery of what it must sometimes *feel* like to be a journalist — a shit! There's no problem at all in forgetting the human part I've enjoyed and exploited while plotting and writing the 'objective' appraisal. An important lesson, this — not a task I'll undertake many times.

News reaches me that a chapel meeting is due to take place to discuss the engagement of a currently celebrated women's lib writer onto the paper. (Apparently there's a separate NUJ chapel for The Sunday Times alone instead of a chapel for all the Thomson newspapers throughout the country. "It's the ship deserting the sinking rat!") The general opinion is that management has over-reached itself and tried to get her in through the back door. "I know all about this because I got in on a fiddle myself though you mustn't believe everything I say. They told me you need three years minimum experience in the provinces; but there are exceptions to that if you're a specialist writer and I got hired as a specialist in industrial law — industrial relations that is with special reference to industrial law. Of course the union said 'Ho ho! no such thing. We've heard of industrial relations but what law?' 'Ho ho!' says I, 'have you ever had an industrial relations bill before? Still not convinced? All right,' I says, 'I may be wrong but let me work for six months on The Sunday Times and then you can decide.' So, I wrote stuff no one could understand, conducted seminars up and down the country and then, finally, pleaded my case on the basis that, though it's outrageous that I'm here — I'm here! And from that moment on I was determined to see that no one like me ever got in again so I at once became a union leader."

I guess that the wit is for my benefit but it's one of those doubletake revelations: 'I want to tell you this but don't take any notice of me telling you.' Still, it doesn't hide the genuine conflict between a real problem of unemployment in the profession where journalists want to maintain openings for their colleagues, and their generous desire not to smother talent. Both sides play around with each other and manoeuvre to save face. In the final confrontation the shrewd, calm NUJ official says to management: "Well, we can't black her copy, we don't want a strike, but if you push me against the wall I'll have to do it. So, what's to be the compromise?" "At which point," staff reports of management, "the management jumps up in great relief and offers, grateful to be let off the hook, one: no one new to be employed for a year; two: no sackings; three: no dismissals without consultations with the unions." It sounds as though management have given away nothing and we can eagerly await her first assault.

> "It's not a pleasant spectacle seeing journalists in a bar boast of how they've revealed to the world the way in which they saw seventeen people die that day at the hands of fascist beasts."

Business News covers a large area of the fourth floor, a newspaper on its own which alone brings in £3 million a year from advertising.* They can't be wholly subversive about the hands which feed them and though they like to present a Bolshie image to the world they're not really open to the suggestion of an alternative to a capitalist system. The establishment need have little fear of the brilliant left-wingers lurking behind the columns of news and views, it will take more than The Sunday Times to crack the ramifications of this country's

* This figure will obviously have increased since 1971.

deeply entrenched and widely accepted competitive spirit. "One is more likely to fumble towards a desirable state through a competitive society than an autocratic one." I'm not sure I understand why these are the only two alternatives to consider, but journalists do enjoy talking with each other even though they frequently don't listen to each other. The stream of words is exuberant and endless. They remind me of those barrack-room lawyer types one met in the forces — full of opinions about everything, everyone, everywhere.

"The civil service is capable of responding to orders but they argue too brilliantly with ministers who are not sufficiently clear on their own ideas . . . The lawyer by definition is a nihilist because if he's great, he says 'my job is to defend people to the law not the law to people' . . . But much more important than the shareholders was that the public was swindled, shareholders deserve what they get, trying to make money work for them instead of working for themselves . . . People who fuck up the system appeal to me . . . He's 65, lives in Switzerland and is the only man I know who can reach into his back pocket and produce enough cash to buy a company. Made his money out of a cheap record-changing device, £20 million, and has just emerged from opulent retirement to make a bid for BSA. Started off by imagining he could make his fortune out of surgical machinery but did what few others did which is he actually took the trouble to get himself qualified as a surgeon in order to test whether his inventions worked. Very strange man, hates unions. He's an elitist fascist but not wholly without charm . . . I agree! £400 million paid back to the international banks leaving £500 millions to pay means nothing to the man in the street. Who can comprehend that? They only know that the rich get richer and the poor get poorer. But, today, poverty is your own fault, today you can stand on your own two feet, anyone can become Prime Minister. Our beloved leader has proved it, the nasty Chancellor

has proved it; all of them self-made and nasty men
saying you too can also all be self-made and nasty
men . . ."

A telephone rings: "There's a lunatic negotiator for the TGWU up in the Midlands who, because he's so bored with the usual demands of his head office, believes that every new contract he draws up on behalf of his workers has got to have at least one original clause in it. This time he's insisted that every man get a day off on his birthday. Anybody interested?" It is difficult to trace the pattern of what's happening. As with every other department it seems that all they do is read newspapers. "Even on the fourth day," I'm assured, "you will think that the paper can't possibly appear." But empty desks hint at journalists out on a job, and the fact that pulls of copy keep coming up from 'the stone' suggests someone has done some writing somewhere at sometime. Even so, how is it all covered? As I linger on they build for me a picture of the vast industrial and economic network. Industry: sub-divided into heavy, light, state-owned and private. Economic management. Industrial relations. International monetary control. The stock market. Take-overs and the interpretation of balance sheets. The impact of new technology. And most of those headings are multiplied, and hence complicated, when dealt with on an international scale. Can they be handled responsibly by such a small staff even though most are first class honours graduates? (One journalist is pointed out as having a double first in classics, "went straight to the Financial Times".) There can be no complaint that they know nothing about industry from the inside, many come from industry and at least one left a number two job on Business News to spend two years in Industry which he gave up in disgust to return to the paper in a less senior position.

I catch myself enjoying their company. It's partly that sardonic tone with the double edges which repel and compel at the same time, but it's also because these

77

weeks in The Sunday Times offices remind me of the pleasures of working with people instead of the terrifying, paranoia-making isolation of working alone at home. ("There's a plot afoot to rehabilitate Arnold Wesker," writes one journalist in The Guardian, reviewing my book of short stories and a good, critical study of my plays, which throws me into a new fit of paranoia as I sit at home working on this piece.)

> "The elegant sneer is admired and if it's like Pope it's very good indeed. Problem is it's rarely like Pope."

Weinstock is the glamour boy of the moment and I hear him discussed endlessly. It's obviously imperative to read the profile on him to discover what there is about shop-keepers that excites and mesmerises the intelligent journalists of Business News. "When Weinstock came into GEC via an 8.5 million takeover of his father-in-law's firm, Radio and Allied, his prime task was to weed out waste." A gardener! "There was waste in design . . . There was £10 million (at a time when GEC had £20 million overdraft) tied up in 32 now scrapped regional headquarters!" So? Weinstock tidied it up, big deal! Is big business so badly run that when a man comes along and does, for a great deal of money, simply what he's supposed to do, he's called a genius? A quartermaster, that's all! Finally, when all is said and done, he'll contribute nothing more to our understanding of pain or other men, he'll add nothing beautiful to the world. He's not even an inventor, just a tidy-upper who can resist the need to be loved; an efficient, money making man, but hard, who has no qualms about sacking and ordering men around; which is not his fault, he'll say, because the world demands efficiency, men depend upon it, someone must pay the price. Very convenient.

78

But, it can't be anything so simple that commands the respect of Business News journalists. Perhaps it is that though Weinstock appeals to men's sense of greed he must, paradoxically, elicit from them a high degree of cooperation in order to satisfy that greed. The men under him must work unselfishly for their privileges. "This continuous dialogue between Stanhope Gate (Weinstock's headquarters) and the companies is dedicated to uncovering the truth in each situation. Business men like running away from unpleasant facts. But Weinstock's approach," writes our good business journalist, "is exactly that of a good business journalist, determined to cut through half truths and vague generalisations. One of his great strengths is that he never believes anything, and himself says 'all information is suspect'." It is left to the sardonic voice of another good business journalist to cap the Weinstock image. "Arnold Weinstock's attitude is rather like that of the baron of whom it was asked: why do you build your walls so high and strong? To which he replied: in order to give the peasants' hovels something to lean upon."

Yet alongside the journalist eulogising Weinstock's iron hand is the journalist rushing to defend the humanity of The Sunday Times management. "As for how ruthless we are, huh! Do you know we had a woman on the travel page who regularly, for two years, used to write a piece saying such and such a place was a lovely sunny beach until the Jews got there! Two years! We never printed it of course but it took us two years before she was sacked. And the ———'s editor! Terrible man! But it took us seven years to pluck up the courage to retire him at 53 on a pension plus a paying consultancy job for five years. Yet there are nice, liberal men on The Observer who are beastly to each other, awful!"

My favourite story about Business News is of the time everyone was trying to find a name for the business gossip column. At last someone came up with the name of Prufrock which, most seemed to recall, was the name of a tough, respectable business man in an Eliot poem.

Twenty-four hours before going to press the editor asked 'why and who, Prufrock?' And the poem was proudly brought out:

"No! I am not Prince Hamlet, nor was meant to be;
Am an attendant lord, one that will do
To swell a progress, start a scene or two,
Advise the prince; no doubt, an easy tool,
Deferential, glad to be of use,
Politic, cautious, and meticulous;
Full of high sentence, but a bit obtuse;
At times, indeed, almost ridiculous —
Almost, at times, the fool.
I grow old . . . I grow old . . .
I shall wear the bottoms of my trousers rolled.
Shall I part my hair behind? Do I dare to eat a peach?
I shall wear white flannel trousers, and walk upon the
    beach.
I have heard the mermaids singing each to each.
I do not think that they will sing to me."

After the silence there followed agonising hours while everyone stamped around through other books and poems and Roget's Thesaurus trying to find a new name until, weary, they decided, inappropriate or not, Prufrock, damn it, was a good name.

> "Fink is an abusive term for someone upon whom the journalist relies for his information. The name reveals our love-hate relationship with our job."

Someone from Insight comes down to Business News and reports: "I've just had an earbending fink on the telephone who says he's got damaging documents which will implicate Mr. A." "Oh," says a sweet looking, baby-faced but bearded financial tipster, "are we rubbishing Mr. A? He's a con man but we all love him; he's the most charming con man in the food industry, if that's what you can call it." They say they'll see the fink and I ask whether I can be in at the meeting. They say with pleasure! if the fink doesn't mind. The next day he arrives with a friend. I remind the journalists that I want to attend and they ask the fink. My guess is that he doesn't quite hear what their request is and imagines I'm simply another journalist — he says yes.

The fink's story

He says, with that jocular English modesty (which, with zany irrelevance, makes me think the English could never be avant-garde about anything because they're too hearty) he says: "I'm a plumber," when what he means is he's an engineer. The basis of his story, which I listen to with total incredulity my eyes growing wider and wider each moment much to the amusement, I suspect, of the two journalists, is this: he had discovered, after minute research, that Mr. A's stated share price since 1967 was based on a false market and that Mr. A was able to achieve this through a complicated system of interlocking holdings which worked roughly in this way; the English company takes over a French company which is then able to buy shares in the subsidiary of the English company which then buys . . . and so on. The Sunday Times journalists sit patiently and listen. They do so for three hours, committing themselves to little more than an observation about A being "our favourite crook" while concentrating mostly on pertinent questions that will draw out the fink's motives. He seems to have done a fantastic amount of research and from his briefcase produces balance sheets as published in the Financial Times and graphs he's drawn based on those balance sheets. "And there's this woman in high French financial circles who's also managing director of his French company — running with the hare and hunting with the hounds — so it's all open and conforms absolutely with the letter and spirit of French law, which isn't saying much, and it all looks lovely, a respected housekeeper at the top, very attractive."

I begin to feel pleased with myself that I can understand so much about high finance and then he utters his first give-away. "Of course I bought his shares at 71 and sold them at 93 on the basis of what I knew he was going to do. I'd been following him so closely that I understood his pattern of behaviour, his psychology as it were." Well, I think, *that's* not nice Mr. Fink. At half time I break to ask if they want any drink, coffee or something. They say they would like anything liquid. The secretaries are reluctant to supply me, offering excuses like "no clean cups, no water in the kettles, no milk". I return, defeated and apologetic, but it's not my house. Ten minutes later, however, a secretary appears with a tray of coffee. "I was overcome with remorse," she says.

He continues producing his crowded sheets of figures and graphs and talks with a growing agitation that's sexual, as though he's making love to his theme. Elegant arm, hand and finger gestures describe in the air the patterns of his research. The journalists stop him to suggest here and there flaws in his case, which he concedes but balances with more and more evidence. "The mafia in all this is snuff," he says. "Oh, don't laugh, don't laugh." He reaches into his briefcase for cuttings from German magazines. "Snuff is the new narcotic, you can put your LSD in it and the kids in Germany and Sweden are all taking it up." Where is it all leading? His saga seems many-vaulted and endless. Then, for no apparent reason he tells the story of a well-known banker giving money to two old people in order to help them set up a chocolate factory. A straight forward account except that he refers to the old people as being "two Jews from Vienna". I tell myself to sit still and not be so sensitive. But I notice The Sunday Times men refer, with too deliberate a care I feel, not to the 'Jews from Vienna' but to 'those Viennese immigrants'. Then he says how a friend of his sees Mr. A constantly in the company of Mr. B and C — both well known Jewish financiers. Then he talks about another character in his saga as "an old German Jew". At which point they try to get him away from such asides and ask: "It must be very frustrating never having met the man?"

"Good lor no!" he replies. "I don't ever want to meet him. I'm so dead against him that I'm frightened of being seduced by his charm. It's much better this way. I've read a file on him *this* thick, and I've followed his manoeuvrings this way and that, watched how he's approached first this one for capital, then moved to that one, then tried another attack and realised there's nothing to be gained and so moved on. I've watched him wheedling back and forth and studied his mentality, looked at his handwriting, lived with his thinking for six months — oh no! I know him much better this way. I know him *intimately*."

His excitement reaches a climax, he's been listened to so well and attentively, been so praised for his research that his guard lowers and, his eyes agitated by a sinister intelligence, he confesses his passion: "I'm obsessed by the European Jewish Mafia and I've been reading about them going as far back to the time when Napoleon freed the Jews. I mean, think about it, there's the tightly knit X's family together with Y and Z on the continent, and Messrs. A, B and C on this side of the channel, and with the common market round the corner . . ." He brings his two hands together, locking elegant curled fingers into elegant curled fingers. ". . . click! The opportunity they've been waiting for — a highly closed plot in the traditional Jewish manner. But I'm not," he adds, "at all anti-semitic. Only you must see that they're trying to dominate the new and most important areas of leisure and food."

I can't stay to hear more. The description of the plot has already made me late for a dinner date. It's been frightening; all the more so because the fink's data has been persuasive and seems to have made complete financial sense to the two Sunday Times experts. The next day I can't wait to confront them and ask: "Well, what do you propose to do about the Jewish plot to dominate the world?" The journalists are very cool. "The problem is, if the company declares an overseas profit of £1 million they don't have to say where it comes from. What we have to do is prove there's been rigging of the Stock Exchange and the only people who can do that are the Stock Exchange Council who can ask to look at the records of the jobbers. And they'll only do this if a company is folding or if the government asks for an investigation. On the other hand," the journalists observe, "don't you always do business with your friends? Who else do you do it with? That's what business is about."

The fink fascinates me and I make my own investigations sharing even more the excitement of being a journalist, 'naming the guilty men'. I discover the fink worked for a large foreign company as what they call a spare brain. He'd been with them for ten years advising them on re-organisation and investments while at the same time making a great deal of money from his own speculations. He was finally sacked when it was discovered he was making very long 'phone calls on the company's account to far away places in pursuit of those speculations. I pass this on to the journalists. Weeks later The Sunday Times report on their investigation into Mr. A and conclude that everything seems to be above-board.

I understand why it's such an absorbing world, the business world, murky though it is. It's obvious the business section is prevented from reporting everything and I keep hearing about how Maxwell was unfortunate but that in fact, compared with some of the men and goings-on in the city, he was an amateur fallen angel. I learn, and must remember, to distinguish between industrialists, bankers and stockbrokers. The first consider themselves the real workers and mistrust city men as parasitical speculators. Though for their almost total indifference to human happiness, except in so far as it produces for them employees who are more

84

manipulable, my fascination ends with wishing a plague on all their houses.

Part Four

"The system is awful. You can even make up the quotes. It's like being in front of a firing squad. Your victim can *ask* to see the copy but not legally so."

Censorship

I become interested in a reporter's article on the plight of low-paid workers; he's excited to have discovered from government sources, that they will need pay rises of 42% a year if their standard of living is not to fall. In his eagerness to attack "thirteen years of Tory misrule" his problem is to avoid his article becoming too strident. How can he offer the facts and figures and be certain their implications are understood? He confesses to operating an in-built censorship and tones down the article; then, to his pleasure, discovers he's under-done it. His seniors tell him not to mess about, it's a shocking state of affairs and they want to say so. The sentence: "From this point on the only item which chips away at increased earnings is income tax" is changed to the more sharply worded: "From this point on only income tax continues to bite more deeply into increased earnings."

The question of censorship inevitably emerges. There's a difference of opinion. Someone says Lord Thomson doesn't interfere: "He's so scrupulous about the entire Times Newspaper organisation that, despite owning 85% of the shares and Astors only 15%, when he appointed an outside set of directors he gave Astors an equal say on who those directors should be." Someone else cries: "Nonsense! It's just this outside body that exerts more pressure than anyone else. Whenever I'm interviewing X he never fails to remind me that he's a director of The Sunday Times." Another reporter tells the story of how: "I once had a 'phone call from Thomson to give me a story about the struggle going on between Occidental Petroleum and another company over drilling rights in the Persian Gulf. The head of

Occidental is also a friend of Thomson and Thomson rang me up three times on the Saturday to make sure I was representing the Occidental's story and urging that the British Government should come down on Occidental's side. Mind you he wasn't urging me to write what I didn't want to — but what if he were?" Someone answers very sharply and firmly: "Nothing would happen! Because *we* decide the journalism ourselves. We're not above taking any news tip from Lord Thomson; and we're not afraid to ignore one."

I check that among the directors are: Sir Kenneth Keith of Hill Samuel — merchant bankers; Lord Shawcross, Chairman of the Takeover Panel; Sir Eric Roll the economist and a director of the Bank of England; Sir George Pope, ex-manager of The Times; Sir Donald Anderson, ex-Chairman of P&O Shipping Lines; Lord Robens, ex-Chairman of the National Coal Board. "Ah ha!" I say, "men outside the running of the newspaper but hardly outside the system." "That's the old conspiracy theory," someone says. It's true, and as I don't hold it I'm embarrassed to be caught uttering it. I try to rebalance myself. "But surely it's acknowledged that there are accepted means of them 'letting it be known that . . .'?" "You have a concept of 'them' and 'us'," I'm told. "Who's 'them'? No person, no organisation can be monolithic. The idea that an administrative group of men can possibly share a single simple view of the world is nonsense."

I didn't want to have to defend a conspiracy theory I didn't believe in; though I do believe that when the fundamental laws of competitive society are challenged then property, privilege and private enterprise, without needing to share a 'simple view of the world', close ranks. Not that a socialist can draw a complacent comfort from *that* simple analysis; the conflict is often confused in that the challengers (revolutionaries) seem so frequently to attract the worst demagogues, opportunists and fervourists of violence into their ranks that the poor 'people', in whose name all is done, are left with little but the two hells from which to choose. But I digress.

Someone rushed to defend the purity of the paper. "I could tell you about every one of those Board members showing how we'd printed stories which went counter to the interests of the Thomson organisation. There was the time when we reported that the government in British Guyana had got in with the help of the C.I.A. — and at that moment a team of Thomson's men were there negotiating for the TV franchise which of course they didn't get because they got blamed, wrongly, for the story. But *we* didn't hear a murmur from Thomson. Came back to us as a joke years later. Then there was the time there was talk of handing over a second TV channel to I.T.V., the original source of a lot of Lord Thomson's money. We opposed it! Sunday Times came right out against it! Not a murmur. And the time the colour magazine published some photographs of poor conditions for blacks in South Africa? The managing director of Thomson Organisation had his business facilities withdrawn but we heard not a single complaint from him. And what about that 'Justice' report criticising the judiciary? Lord Shawcross wrote to The Times condemning us and he, don't forget, is a director, one of those men you mention as being 'hardly outside the system'. But we published and he made his protest in public. There are countless examples. No! If anything, we're perverse in the way we bend over backwards to maintain our purity. In fact we so want to demonstrate our impartiality we're often in danger of being unfair to those closest to us!"

I wander up to have coffee with my first day's guide, a pipe-smoking, sardonic man, and tackle him on the question of pressures from above: "I suppose there does exist a kind of collective wisdom which might be biased in some kind of way because of confrontation with commercial influences." He sucks on his pipe, thoughtfully, as though he's interested himself in his own observation. Then: "No," he changes his mind. "That's a little naughty of me." I pursue him: "Look, I've never really believed in the conspiracy theory — the English capitalist system is too well established to need a conspiracy — but a newspaper like The Sunday Times must sometimes find itself confronted by a dilemma between its responsibility to print a story and a government warning about the consequences." "Mmm — yes — it does happen," he talks like a landmine, unobtrusively; you don't believe such a peaceful, pipe-sucking landscape can explode; "but on other papers, not this one. There are checks and balances you see, outside the system — the ecological balances of Whitehall, public opinion and the law; laws of privacy, of libel, of contempt. Like a fish in a pond, really. All you do is try to be a pretty good fish. Danger comes when fishes want to be birds." There's no controlling a good explosion.

Ah well! Institutions, it seems, are like people — you must live with them on an intimate level in order to discover their truths. Journalism's pure and virgin daughter was The Sunday Times — if I really wanted to know her vices and virtues, if I really feared that journalism's lady of justice had lapses of honesty or succumbed to after dinner seductions at the friendly tables of power then I should marry her myself and find out. But what journalist ever wedded *his* story — indeed it had been given me as an adage of journalism that if you became too involved with your subject you lost objectivity. Not that I accept the proposition of 'objectivity' — who but God?

I see Business News through to the end of the week. It's in this part of the paper where they ask me, with anxious good humour, if I'm preparing a report for the editor, and where I first hear the rumour that "he's not writing a play at all but a series of articles for The Observer". I tell everyone that I'm toying with the idea of writing a kind of Insight on The Sunday Times but that it might be only for the internal amusement of the Staff. Secretly I hope to produce an inspired piece which the editor can't resist or feels challenged to print. The wish to write a major piece of journalism has been nagging me for some time now — perhaps this will be it.

The last moments with Business News are touching.

We go into the editor's office. "Well," he says, "I think we've got a very good business news tonight. That piece by ——, a great improvement, seems to get better each week, don't you think?" Soft glows of satisfaction appear, barely hidden by hearty remarks aimed at showing they didn't really hear the praise. The editor's in a good mood and distributes some of the praise in the direction of himself. "We're the only ones who've really dared to go to town on the Spanish cholera epidemic." And it's true, four columns seven inches high, plus a large map showing the cholera's movement. Very dramatic. But when I receive my own copy on the following morning the layout's changed. Why? Because on the Saturday they have read in an early edition of The People that Wilson is telling all about his financial state and his overdraft, and this important information is given place of honour at the top of the page while the editor's pride — the cholera spread — is cut; the map is gone and with it a column of copy. After the editor's bouquet-handing-out meeting I say to them: "Well, that was sweet and comforting, no complaints from the ed." "Oh," they say, brushing aside a need to acknowledge this, "it's so depressing. The competition is so bad, so lazy. I mean look at The Observer on IPC. They've asked no questions, done no homework, just looked at today's Financial Times and made a couple of 'phone calls. They've sent no one out to see anyone. It's so bad."

"We're a bundle of news for a bundle of family. Each section can be used by different parts of the family. Doesn't matter if papa buys us for the business news as long as his wife is happy with the review section and kids fight over the supplement."

Foreign

Here is where I really feel at the centre of the world. The telex tape ticks and pumps out the world's trials and tribulations; but no one is satisfied they can do the job of reporting foreign news adequately. "It's too costly. We have a London office staff of four and two secretaries plus the part-time services of the paper's major feature writers; an overseas staff of five, plus a hundred foreign correspondents of varying ability whom we share with other papers and call 'stringers'." I work out that it costs about £257,000 to run the entire foreign wing for a year even though they've got no full-time man in Latin America, Africa, Eastern Europe, Moscow, the Far East or the Middle East. But a fascinating and perhaps more vivid reporting comes from unprofessional contacts who work in international business, political or social organisations.

A 'phone call comes through from someone to say he's got a trunk load of documents revealing the real truth about Biafra. "Boy, just wait till you see what's inside this trunk, you've never really seen a story like this one, boy this is really a big one." They sigh. "If only he knew how sick we were of going through trunks full of documents telling 'the real truth' about Biafra. When we asked shall we meet in his flat he said 'Oh no! better be somewhere where no one can see us'. Trouble is you never know about these people, although our experience is that it's usually the man who rings up and says 'I don't suppose this will be of any interest to you' who produces the most shattering documents."

Here, more than in any other department of the newspaper are to be found extraordinary pressures. Chance meetings with people who have been at the centre of world events can produce revelations of hair-raising horrendousness which, when certain powers get wind of them, produce threats to the life and family of the informant who is the one person who can finally sign to the truth of the information; and after months of investigation involving great expense and energy, the story has to be abandoned. "Suddenly the sky is dark with flying lawyers."

A pursuit of fact thoroughly supported by evidence inspires a less flippant tone in these offices than elsewhere. The observations of Business News that the Maxwell affair was insignificant compared to the other goings on in the city meet with stern rebuff here. "I can't believe they really think that. Maxwell was an M.P. involved in deals worth nine millions — near to getting a cabinet post and bidding for two national newspapers, that's not insignificant." I ask someone else (not from the Foreign department) whether Pergamon would have collapsed with its attendant miseries for shareholders (about whom he seemed concerned) if they'd not done their investigation into the affair. "Good question. We don't know. We *think* he'd have gone under even without our enquiries, but who knows?"

Is there feedback from their investigations? "We're in the business of producing information rather than results; can't confuse the two or you end up with bad, emotional copy which weakens the credibility of the piece by its pleadings. There's only one issue which we've really gone to town on in order to produce results and that's Pakistan. The editor wants us to go on and on every week until something is done, even at the risk of becoming boring. And for a newspaper editor that's brave, don't you think?" Yes, I do think, but I want to know more, because if they don't produce results of some sort then they must surely be forced to look at the way they're conducting this 'business of producing information'. I'm told the story of an important Sunday journalist who became so involved in the Ulster crisis that she ended up organising and leading Catholic committees. I expressed great sympathy and admiration for such an action; it makes the journalist very human to have turned from observation to commitment. Her stories will now have real insight and an honestly declared bias. "*If* she wrote stories. But now she can't. The two can't be mixed."

An M.P. regarded five years ago as one of the bright young hopes in the Labour Party comes up as a topic of conversation. It's recalled that he'd held a junior minister's post from which he'd resigned. But though he's considered a friend by five members of the staff, yet they take time to remember which ministry it is and no one can remember what issue he'd resigned over.

"Poor bloke," says one, "he probably sweated over his decision for months and now no one remembers what it is."

"Oh, I don't know. He probably thought he'd get his token resignation over and done with while he was still in only a junior post."

"Still," they muse, "we don't remember. It's revealing."

I'm asked if I've found out where the power lies in the newspaper. It's an innocent question which suddenly brings into focus the submerged patterns of fighting egos. I don't envy the Captain who has to control this team of brilliantly intimidating social terrorists.

A stranger comes in to try and persuade them that Agnew's impending visit to Greece is an important moment to write a story which gathers together and reveals the growing anti-junta pressures that exist. They listen carefully to his arguments: there's the pressure of the U.S. Congress to cut off arms supplies; rebellious parliaments in Bonn and Denmark — members of the North Atlantic Assembly, and even the American embassy in Athens is cold towards their Greek hosts. The foreign team are uncertain and pummel him with incisive questions.

"We don't *really* know how isolated Greece is, do we? Is U.S. support for them *really* collapsing? None of these things have actually happened. I mean we don't know and, with all respect, you don't know either."

The stranger stands up to them well matching intelligence for intelligence.

"Only a minority of officers are behind the junta. If the majority had to choose between the Western

Alliance and the junta they'd choose Western Alliance."

"Do we have anyone inside Greece who could produce concrete evidence to prove this?"

"We have contacts who can support the view but not provide the evidence."

"Because you see, we get so many people telling us how this or that country's regime doesn't have the support of its peoples but little ever happens or looks as though it could happen."

I can't resist asking them about the rumours that spies inhabit the foreign department of the newspaper. What can they say? *They* wouldn't know. "It's in the nature of something secret that it's kept secret." Of course! But I enjoy the gentle blush that comes to their faces full of studious indifference. "One thing is for certain, absolutely, the editor wouldn't hire anyone knowing he was employed by any secret service organisation." It's an oddly naive thing to say. On the other hand they don't doubt that after a correspondent has been somewhere, or it's known he's going, they call him to lunch and ask him about his trip. "But most journalists would tell them to fuck off or just have lunch and simply tell them what they'd just written in their articles." What was suspected, however, was that certain overseas stringers who seemed to have acquired large houses and extraordinarily lavish interiors on mere journalists' salaries were also possibly used by intelligence agencies. But much more likely the rumour probably began because Ian Fleming was once foreign manager of The Sunday Times; or perhaps because everyone drew dark conclusions from the fact that Philby once wrote for The Observer and The Economist. Yer pays yer money and takes yer pick.

There are sad moments. A reporter has just struggled to knock his largest ever story down from 4,000 to 2,500 words. With modest and expectant pride he asks one of his colleagues, a poker-faced heavyweight 'with an aggressive intelligence and great personal kindness': "Well, what d'you think?" The piece is a frolicking account of the problems encountered in an assortment of channel crossings. Our unsmiling heavyweight had responsibility for, and had himself succeeded in pushing out space to accommodate, someone else's account of the Libyan counter-coup. Bigger stuff, of course. Not your tender, minor witticisms about family travel, no! More important your cruelly damaging pontifications upon political thuggery. The lightweight waits for the heavyweight to comment. "Reasonable, reasonable," he says.

I at once become interested in how the Libyan counter-coup is written. The Business News team have been sending it up.

"It's the classic Insight story, a parody of itself. 'At 00.11 hours a BOAC Viscount Flight 0752 took off from Heathrow . . .' "

Someone else picks up the story. " 'At the same time a Russian Illyshin military trainer crashed inside Iraq territory killing all the Iraqi military passengers . . .' "

" 'Who can't sue of course and neither can the executed Sudanese coup officers . . .' "

" 'Philby at that moment was eating his first hard boiled egg in the Moscow restaurant . . .' "

" 'Four minutes, naturally . . .' "

" 'Meanwhile, the Prime Minister in Malta . . .' "

" 'At first sight all these far-flung incidents have no connection . . .' And the awful thing is that the bloody story reads so well."

It is, as was bitchily forecast, a predictable Insight piece: a detective-like assembly of facts reading in that low-tone American voice of mock instant drama — it's happening now, readers, as I write, this very moment. But the great political judgement at the end is rather like a schoolboy's triumphant ending to his studiously researched essay answering the question: 'The VC 10 was hi-jacked by Libya because Arab unity was at stake. Comment.' The article throws in a wide range of facts showing how hard the student has worked. "The Libyan leader is an Arab visionary," the article dramatically announces and then concludes, to my surprise, in the language of self-satisfied sixth-form scholarship: ". . .

and that is why (dear teacher?) on Thursday morning he forced down the BOAC airliner to remove from it the two men who in his eyes were determined to undermine his personal vision of Arab unity by their secular challenge." Yes, I think to myself, truly great stuff, and then I say — stop being bitchy, this particular heavy-weight is one of the best minds on the paper. I'd just read his private memo to the committee on privacy — a responsible and cogently argued document in defence of the journalist's duty to investigate 'secret and well protected misbehaviour' of a political or social — not private — kind.

But what can I do? I find myself thrown violently between respects and derisions for the journalist's manner; and it occurs to me that perhaps the people are better than their product. For example, after the brave fight put up for the retention of the female liberationist I, as well as thousands of others, look forward to her first article. And here she comes, out of the clouds, swooping down to make her first low-level attack on a product central to the cause of woman's liberation. Guess what? Vaginal deodorants! How imaginative of editorial to recognise such a talent. How courageous of The Sunday Times, so dependent upon advertising for its survival, to jecpardise potential revenue from advertising space bought by manufacturers of 'alternative female smells'. On the other hand, the record is impressive: Rachman, Cornfeld, Pergamon, Pakistan, Belfast. And weeks later, I read a finely argued piece of demolition called 'The Myth of The Silent Majority' which makes the simple point that the convenience of such a concept of silence is — the silence. If you say nothing then anybody can claim to speak for you. Such an article vindicates all journalism and if any debate opens on the strengths and weaknesses of the profession it could do worse than centre around the question why all journalism is not of such a level of writing.

"The essence of journalistic investigation is that it should usually concern matters which cannot be left to the police, or to other official bodies — sometimes it may be the police or official bodies that should be investigated. There is perhaps no other country where the administration of society is carried out more honestly, humanely and conscientiously than in Britain. That does not mean that we have a society so perfect that we can afford to limit democratic scrutiny."

Sports

Now, here is a proud and energetic section. Proud because "until recently sports journalists were bottom on the rung of journalists, unless they were gentleman journalists. They were either simply fans, failed performers or bad writers on other parts of the paper. Today our aims are almost the contrary — we would sooner produce better written than comprehensive copy." Energetic for two reasons; the first being the obvious organisation needed throughout the week to despatch so many freelancers over the country to cover the endless sporting events of this sporting isle. The second, more interesting; everyone is an 'expert' on sport. All sports departments suffer from the I'll-catch-you-game. 'Phone calls and letters are insistent and constant. Dealing in Everyman's preoccupation I expect to encounter cockiness. Not so. "Sports writers are always feeling guilty for not covering something more important, more useful. Classic example? The golf reporter covering golf in Ulster. What the hell was he doing covering golf in *Ulster*?"

My own attitudes to sport are ambivalent: disgust at the animal aggression of boxing mixed with admiration for its skill and physical endurance; fear of the hysterical football crowds mingled with a marvelling at their knowledge of the game; wonder at athletic feats alongside my personal boredom with even a minimal pursuit of bodily exercise. I decide to face the sports boys with what I believe is the safe side of my ambivalence. Thinking of my feeble muscles, stiff, complacent bones and loathsome little paunch I defend the healthy body/healthy mind approach. Their response shatters and diminishes. "Sport is a fascist activity in that it's governed by rules against which there is no appeal and which, if applied to a democratic society, could not be upheld. What's more fascist than all that crap about a healthy body a healthy mind, and character being built on the playing fields of Eton? All balls. *What* character? That's the point." That'll teach me to abandon my instincts and run with the hounds.

Still, I work out a defence for a relationship between an alert body and an alert mind. They give me no quarter. "What great writer do you know ran a couple of miles before picking up a pen? A quarrel with his wife is more likely to stir him, a bit of private distress — that'll sharpen his emotions, not a handful of physical jerks." Don't I know this is true, why am I arguing? Yet I continue feebly about how fresh and prepared for anything one can be after a walk or a swim. "If you're an idiot not even an Olympic medal changes that fact," they reply. They've misunderstood, thank God! I tell them that I'm not suggesting a healthy body *made* a healthy mind but that given a lively mind to begin with it was enhanced by a fit body. They grudgingly concede the possibility.

I ask if different sports produce a different public. "Rugby crowds are fair-minded and less violent because the violence is played out on the pitch. Wimbledon audiences tend to favour the underdog, love to see the leading player beaten. Some think there's violence in soccer crowds only when it's mirroring the violence of a particular game. Golf? All golfers are conservative and reactionary because the roots of their playing begin in the country clubs, crowds must be the same. But as soon as a sport is gambled over then the response of the crowd is uglier - boxing's a good example." I remember later that I could have pointed to the pastoral quality of horse-racing crowds.

My biggest delight is to have an old idea of my own confirmed. "No sports centre should be built without arts facilities, and vice versa." This idea is typical of their imaginative approach. "We're not simply concerned with reporting sports events, we cover the sporting society also." The narrow approach I'd expected is completely exploded. "We'd even love to change over to the arts pages for six months."

They give me a momentary guilt. "Why have you left us till last?" It's not that they're resentful but feel it confirms their own view of themselves. "We're the least important I suppose?" I assure them it's partly the way it worked out and partly a reflection of my own ignorance of and scant interest in the subject — "not a value judgement". They don't seem convinced.

An industrial dispute occupies much of my days with them. The garage is being closed down because management want to rebuild on the site and economise on staff. Thirty-three men are to be made redundant. The messengers come out in sympathy and copy ceases to flow between departments. Articles are being written which may not be printed. It's a ghostly activity. Confusion exists about who is demanding what. The union says it doesn't want the decision withdrawn but only wants the date for closure postponed. Management say it's postponed the date once already. A document states that the compensation figure is £800. One of the garage men complains he's been told he won't get that sum. Rumour has it that the figure was a misprint. Everyone seems confused and helpless. The Evening Standard give the story to its front page lead and for once, being on the inside, I can see that all they've done is quote from that internal document without making any attempt to get versions of the dispute from a direct confrontation with either management or union. Other journalists and various union representatives are lured to the sports office whose editor is the chapel rep.

"The difference between the production and the creative side is that we're prepared to work at all hours in order to get the paper out whereas production don't care a damn . . . It's a question of whether they want to accept a situation in which 33 men are dismissed now with compensation and facilities for retraining, or whether 2,500 lose their jobs in a few years time. I don't know why they can't see that. The man who can solve human relations problems like that is a genius . . . Basically, as working class men they don't care about the kind of journalism we produce, not that they've really studied it . . . They've stopped the securicor van from bringing in any cash so now the office girls can't be paid. Bloody-minded isn't it? I mean they're only hurting their friends. Don't they know that most of us get paid monthly and the cheques go straight into the bank? . . . It's this comprehensive system. The unions promise increased productivity for higher wages. What happens? The fun goes out of the job. The compositors used to follow through and care about — because they knew about — a sports story. They'd work right through the day. Now they're changed in the course of a day and editorial is faced with different compositors to whom they have to explain the layout all over again. They don't like it any more than we do . . . It's not a normal working class conflict. Those men drive Jaguars and own business on the side which their wives run for the two or three days they're here. They're just protecting their large salaries even at the expense of the rest of us. Do you know a cleaner here earns between £2,000 and £2,500 a year — the minimum salary for a journalist. Others on production can earn as much as £96 a week, more than the journalist's average wage.*

---

* Today's figures: a cleaner earns £3,650 for a 37½ hour week; minimum salary for a journalist is £4,500; a lino operator can gross £200 in a five-day week.

*They're working class capitalists . . . It's not true! All
we're asking is that they withdraw the date of the
25th to give our branches time to discuss the
situation. Now it's a matter of principle for us, and
for management it's a question of personal pride that
they've decided on that date and they don't want to
shift from it. But we've got old men sitting down
there who are terrified about what's going to happen
in terms of pensions. No one's discussed pensions,
pension arrangements are very unsatisfactory on this
paper . . . "*

A staff lawyer comes in to the middle of this sad
confusion to ask what chances there are of them having
a newspaper, he wants to know if he's going to be able
to go to the races or not!

> "You still here? You'd better write that
> play quickly or you'll be writing about a
> defunct activity!"

Conclusions?

The journalist knows his world is among the least
perfect of all imperfect worlds. Most are rearing to get
out and write books — the best of them do, frustrated
by small canvases and the butterfly life of their hard
earned thoughts and words. "Conveyor belt work,
harsh, destructive, written in a hurry. I'm increasingly
irritated by the necessary approximations of journalism."
They can't really be called callous just because they
need the relief of their own humour. "Jesus! What a
background I had! Were you born in a ghetto? You
were? Really? That's true? God, how I resent my father
for being so rich. All the best people were born in a
ghetto; look at Wesker, that's why he was born with a
silver typewriter in his mouth. If only my father had

bought us a ghetto, one we could go to for weekends, now that would have been something!"

Yet, despite such disarming wit I can't rid myself of the suspicion that they seem to *relish* the process of what they expose more than they *care* about what is exposed. A very dubious mechanism is at work when such a large number of people assume for themselves the self-righteous responsibility of interfering to protect society against others whom *they* have decided are interfering and self-righteous. Especially when their own definition of their duty to investigate 'secret and well protected misbehaviour' is such a boomerang. Journalism may not be a secret activity but it is certainly one of the most 'well protected'. Which editor would allow an investigatory profile of his newspaper to appear in his own columns? Certainly a gentleman's agreement prevents them printing damaging information about each other. The sports department once printed two stories about how The Sun manufactured a sports story. The editor of The Sun wrote to his counterpart on The Sunday Times and said 'lay off'.

All motives, even for the serious journalist, are suspect except his own. (I'm not referring to the anonymous little Farts of Fleet Street which every newspaper seems obliged to produce in gossip or comment columns all over the world.) And this makes him like the vicious prison officer whom society also justifies because he appears to be guarding society against its 'undesirables'. Yet, though someone must guard prisons, one is constantly tempted to wonder what kind of mentality opts for the job of ensuring men are deprived of their freedom. Similarly, though someone must guard society from charlatans, exploiters and political fraudulence, yet, one wonders, how carefully are those guards chosen for their wise ability to distinguish between honesty and dishonesty? How 'pure' can the soul be that traffics in human blemishes? And, further, are the pressures of journalism, profit-motivated as they must finally be, conducive to the exercise of perspicacious judgements? Like gladiatorial arenas, newspapers claim to know their audience's taste for blood. Hence little is celebrated, there is no conflict in that act; crucifixion is more dramatic. Although one famous columnist points out how journalism is a flat communicator: "you can't see the face of the man writing the print. Television is much more alive. You can measure what's being said by the manner and face that's saying it. That's *real* conflict — vivid."

But the soul, however insensitive, wearies of destruction; carnage must as well as 'love itself have rest'. An individual, an organisation, a society has a tone of voice, through it you can guess at its nature. What sort of nature lives in the arid, hollow tone of a hunter's horn behind which a smile leers? Society may wish to have its watchdogs, but continuous barking is a noise which, like the drip of the tap, can drive out all feeling with its bleak monotony; and sometimes innocent children are savaged.

But if we look at the difference between literature and journalism it becomes even more complicated. Fact may not be truth, and truth, if it has any chance of emerging, may rest in the need to interpret those facts, and both processes, the fictional and the journalistic, are human and thus imperfect; therefore I must concede as a playwright that art, like journalism, is presumptuous. But has journalism's infinitely smaller canvas the wrong kind of discipline to allow any but a superficial exploration of the complex subjects it chooses to handle? You feel you can argue with literature, temper its vicarious experience with your own. Journalism intimidates because its currency appears to be irrefutable fact and the great myth about himself and his profession to which the journalist succumbs is that he is engaged mainly in the communication of objective fact. But if we view journalism as a chemical compound and break it down we would find the ingredient 'fact' existed in only small quantities and even then lumbered by human impurities.

Journalism	=Investigation or Information or Comment.
Investigation	='facts' conveniently or maliciously leaked + (maybe) the evidence of documents -- both selected and interpreted by journalists.
Information	=selected 'facts' + description, vivid or feeble depending upon individual powers of perception.
Comment	=personal opinions in leaders, reviews, features and gossip columns.

Yet even at the level of fact, which is not a discovery to be sneered at, the manner and amount of research done is questionable; the newspaper's library of old clippings is still the journalist's incestuous bed of primary knowledge; myths, prejudices, distortions and inaccuracies are perpetuated through his continual recourse to that brown-papered past of old copy. The cigarette packet warns that smoking can be a danger to health; no newspaper carries the warning, daily, that 'selective attention to data herein contained can be a danger to your view of the world'.

Still, someone who is not a journalist should be worried about writing a play with such a setting; it could end up contrived. And yet, there is a special part of the artist's experience which is not contrived: he or she has been the journalist's subject, frequently -- as have been many public figures, and it is said of the sadist that only his victim truly understands him. In the end, the journalist, as recipient in a very special way of human experience, is the magnified personality in which drama deals. Though only engaged in handing on fragments of information he or she does so under the apparent omnipotence of daily print, which exaggerates his importance and tempts him to exaggerate pronouncements. The dilemma begins when he finds he can only inform without revealing, which leads him to simplify what is complex and confuse it for clarification; in the process he erodes ardours and enthusiasms, deflates egos so that not vanity but self-confidence cracks, and distorts our image of the world. His tragedy begins when each 'God' he self-righteously topples chips away at his own self respect; the damage he does to others destroys a part of himself, and that's a very familiar state; no writer could find himself alien in that sad territory.

Bishops Road
8th November 1971

Words as definitions of experience

In this essay Arnold Wesker asks: is there an essential vocabulary, a survival kit of about fifty basic words which might sharpen a child's wit against mindless violence, political tyranny, spiritual and emotional exploitation. Wesker argues that a separate school subject be created called 'Definitions of Experience' which would explore the key words and works of our culture.

The essay's questions are ones of cultural literacy. Their relationship to the work begun by Paolo Freire in Brazil is discussed in an appended essay by Richard Appignanesi. Together, these two essays mark the beginning of an important debate on literacy, self-expression and language-teaching, which will concern parents, teachers and writers alike. 75p

The Journalists

"The startling originality of The Journalists is that it takes in the whole caboodle: indeed, given Wesker's privileged peek at The Sunday Times, it is tempting to call it All Harold Evans's Men. . . . What matters is Wesker's ironclad conviction that our Lilliputian society is governed by a need to cut giants down to size and that the press is a major part of that process. . . . There is no denying the play's originality of form or richness of content. I can think of no recent play about the media that raises so many probing questions and that captures so well that blend of light banter and heavy industry that characterizes a newspaper office."
Michael Billington, *The Guardian* £1.00

Both these books are published by Writers and Readers Publishing Cooperative, 233a Kentish Town Road, London NW5 2JT.